Youth
Can
Minister

~

*How Families & Churches Can
Nurture & Release Ministering Youth*

~

Bruce & Lynn
Latshaw

Youth Can Minister
How Families & Churches Can
Nurture & Release Ministering Youth
By Bruce & Lynn Latshaw

©1999 by Bruce & Lynn Latshaw.
All rights reserved. Published 1999.

Published by red Publications
in association with Kairos Communications
red Publications
3224 Appleton Rd.
Landenberg, PA 19350
(610) 255-5073

Cover & interior design by Brian Taylor, Pneuma Books
Set in Congress Light 10/13. This is a Pneuma Book.

Printed in the United States of America
05 04 03 02 01 00 99   7 6 5 4 3 2 1

Publisher's Cataloging-in-Publication
(Provided by Quality Books, Inc.)
Latshaw, Bruce.
      Youth can minister: how families & churches can nurture and
release ministering youth / by Bruce & Lynn Latshaw. – 1st ed.
         p. cm.
         LCCN: 99-96613
         ISBN: 0-9674653-0-3

         1. Church work with youth.   2. Child rearing–Religious
aspects–Christianity.   3. Discipling (Christianity)   I. Latshaw. Lynn.
II. Title.

BV4447.L38 1999   259'.23
                                             QBI99-1425

To order additional copies of this book please contact red Publications
at the address or phone listed above.

We thankfully dedicate *Youth Can Minister* to our two faithful fathers in the faith, Pastors Edwin Miller and Frank Downing, who lovingly mentored us when we were young Christians. Truly they were extensions of the hand and heart of the Great Shepherd to us. Their wise guidance and godly characters set us on straight paths in the Lord. Their unconditional acceptance of our unique qualities as Jesus People established an atmosphere of God's loving acceptance that has enabled us to do the work the Lord called us to do. They took substantial personal and professional risks to trust and release us to minister when most clergymen of their generation would not. Through Pastors Ed and Frank, God demonstrated living examples of adults who love and respect Christian youth. We remain unendingly grateful for the big hearts, wise words, and sacrificial deeds of these warm and patient men of God.

Acknowledgements

We thank our church, Newark Christian Fellowship, for being risk-takers and encouraging us and our church youth. We particularly appreciate: 1) their willingness to pay the price so young ones among us can be equipped and released; 2) their servants' hearts toward all; and 3) their spiritual and financial support of the ministries of East Coast Aflame.

We are deeply grateful for the insightful editing work of Rob Palkovitz and Jason Latshaw. We also thank Brad, Christian, and Mandy Dunn for the valuable questions and comments they provided for the part 2 of this book. Thanks also to Sarah Davies for her editorial suggestions.

We appreciate Brian Taylor at Pneuma Books for his ever-creative and artful design/text layout, and for his patient and wise shepherding of this book through to publication.

Lastly, we thank the young brothers and sisters of East Coast Aflame, whose lives we examine in this book. We thank them for choosing to live and minister Jesus as they do (thus providing us with something valuable to write about!) And we thank them for allowing us to reveal not only their strengths but their weaknesses too, so all may see and know that it is truly the "treasure in the earthen vessels" (2 Cor. 4:7), Christ in us, Who deserves to receive all the glory!

— Bruce and Lynn Latshaw
Coauthors

Foreword

*I*t is a pleasure to recommend *Youth Can Minister: How Families & Churches Can Nurture & Release Ministering Youth*, the new book by my friends Bruce and Lynn Latshaw. I have known Bruce and Lynn, their family, and their church for several years and have seen the increasing grace upon them to challenge and influence the Church regarding our paradigm of youth ministry.

In a day when the failure of program-centered youth ministry is abundantly evident, Bruce and Lynn Latshaw are pioneers charting a path back toward the generational connectedness of the Body of Christ. They show us by their lives, the lives of their children, and the youth of their church that the "generation gap" might be part of the world, but it is not something we have to accept in the Kingdom.

This excellent manual shows the process and lessons they have learned over years of not giving up, believing there must be a better way. Today, the tremendous inner stability and outward ministry success of their children and church stand as the best endorsement anyone could have.

I encourage anyone who has young people in some part of their life to digest the story Bruce and Lynn present here. It is a searchlight, gently helping us find our previous flaws in youth ministry and guiding us to a more healthy future.

— Rob Stearns
Eagles' Wings Ministries / Kairos Communications

Contents

Part 2 *"Youthicizing" Our Churches*

Chapter 7 🎲 Identifying Potential On-Fire Youth   84
Bruce helps you identify youth with Christian leadership potential, produce on-fire youth in the local church, and shape young disciples into released ministers.

Chapter 8 🎲 Cultivating Youth Leaders: A Change of Perspective   96
As ECA's traveling pastor, Lynn explains why adults must shift their thinking and behavior toward Christian youth

Chapter 9 🎲 Youth Need Us:
The Importance of Youth & Adults Relating Together in God   107
Lynn shares practical ways local churches can develop adequate adult mentoring of youth.

Chapter 10 🎲 Challenging Youth to Accept Spiritual Responsibility   112
Bruce recalls ECA's growth out of a challenge he issued to teens in his church to rise up into spiritual responsibility.

Chapter 11 🎲 When in Rome   118
Jason Latshaw challenges those who evangelize youth to examine the cultural distinctions of youth today.

Chapter 12 🎲 Youth Tribe:
A Missionary Approach to Youth Ministry   126
Lynn examines the "language" of today's youth and proposes that youth workers accommodate their efforts accordingly to create a cross-cultural missions outlook.

Chapter 13 🎲 Rethink the Wineskin:
Preparing Your Church for a Youth Invasion   140
Bruce suggests practical changes for congregations to create youth-friendly church environments, encouraging a paradigm shift among church leaders.

Conclusion   162

Youth Can Minister

Introduction

"Stir up the gift of God which is in you
through the laying on of my hands."
2 Tim. 1:6

"When I get big I'm going to take over Pop's job!" exclaimed little three-year-old Jonathan, curled up on my lap in the living room, sucking his finger. We all thought the boy was so cute, piping up about things he was surely too young to understand. Little did we suspect that "out of the mouth of a babe" had just come a prophetic glimpse into the ministry potential Jesus had deposited in this destined-to-minister child.

1

Let's just hope this prophecy isn't fulfilled before the old man (me) is ready to retire!

GOD'S PART

In 2 Tim. 1:6, Paul reminds Timothy of the time he laid hands on his young disciple and imparted spiritual gifting to equip him for leadership ministry. Note that the gift was deposited into Timothy's life by divine initiative, but became operative only through the obedient action of the spiritual parent Paul. Without Paul doing his part, God's gift in Timothy would have remained mere potential. And without God's decision to supply a ministry gift to Timothy, the laying on of hands would not have anointed Timothy for service. It's of course a both-and, not an either-or situation.

The Lord must gift young human lives with spiritual enablements destined to shake the world for Him. His sovereign impartation of gifts is the absolute prerequisite if our kids are to become on-fire ministers of the Lord. Not by might, nor by power, but by the Spirit — through His gifts — will our youth be empowered for ministry. We cannot manufacture gifts in youth if He hasn't provided them.

Although humans have no control over the Lord's choice of spiritual gifts — "He [the Spirit] gives them [gifts] to each one, just as He determines" (2 Cor. 12:11) — it is widely believed that a child born into a Christian family stands in special covenant relationship to God by virtue of his placement in that graced atmosphere of faith: "...for otherwise your children are unclean, but now they are holy [set apart]" (1 Cor. 7:14). Since that is so, then it makes sense that the Lord would be pleased to pour wonderful spiritual raw material — gifts ready to be shaped into ministry excellence — into the children of believing parents. I believe He does this. The Lord does His part. He grants the children of Christian parents enormous ministry potential.

OUR PART

Although God is always faithful to do His part, we parents

and church leaders are not always faithful to do ours. We do not effectively manage the gifts the Lord gives our kids. Like irresponsible prodigals, we squander the Father's treasure in our children.

With fresh zeal born of repentant hearts, we must see our parental duty with a new clarity. We must seize hold of our God-given obligation to shape our children's spiritual raw material into structured opportunities for real spiritual achievement. With determination and creativity we must produce family and church environments designed to stir up the gifts deposited in our kids — the young members of the Church of the future and of the present! We must labor purposefully and wisely to see manifested, in our time, the fulfillment of David's prayer in Psalm 144:12: "Let our sons in their youth be as grown-up plants, and our daughters as corner pillars fashioned as for a palace."

This is often where we fail. A combination of spiritual ignorance and adherence to man-made religious tradition blinds us to our children's need for a church environment that is relevant to them. We vainly hope they will choose to abandon their personal cultural preferences regarding religion and embrace ours. We expect them to conform to a style of church fashioned by leaders from a culture far removed in time and taste from their own.

I believe that expectation has proven wrong. The young are not choosing to join our churches but are developing a private spirituality of their own design. The institutional Church seems vastly irrelevant to their lives — even for those who truly do believe in Christ.

We must do better. And we can — if we will.

We must cry out for God to transform the way we think about youth ministry and the place youth are capable of occupying in our "adult" congregational ministry life. By His creative grace we must reinvent the nature of contemporary youth ministry. We must fearlessly examine substantive changes to our churches if our kids and grandkids are going to find places of significance in them.

We must provide new wineskin youth ministry structures for new generations of the Church.

Every chapter of this book except the eleventh, which is contributed by our son Jason, is written individually by either Lynn or me. Both of us approach youth ministry from our individually blended perspectives as pastors, parents (now grandparents!), and as longtime respectful friends of youth. At the lower right hand corner of the first page of each chapter and next to the page numbers, a "B" or an "L" identifies Bruce or Lynn as that chapter's author.

We've organized our material into two parts. The first, "Raising Ministering Youth", focuses on personal, family, and church influences God has used to shape the young people who founded and now lead East Coast Aflame Youth Ministries. Part 2, "'Youthicizing' Our Churches", examines what works in our own church to reach today's youth. It suggests how churches can rethink contemporary youth ministry and restructure aspects of their congregational life accordingly. Simply put, first we tell you how we did it, then we give you ideas on how you can do it too. We've intentionally written this book in an informal, conversational style that should be readable by youth and adults alike. Our use of the word youth designates people from Generation X — those born between 1961 and 1981 — and from Generation Y (the Millenium Generation) — those born after 1981. Our use of the term *ECA* refers to East Coast Aflame Youth Ministries, the growing youth-reaching organization that has developed through the lives and ministries of youth featured in this book.

We pray that God will use our words to radically transform how the Church thinks about and relates to Christian youth. We want our words to help release a worldwide army of qualified, equipped, anointed youth who, in loving and dynamic partnership with Christian adults, will impact their generation, revive the Church, and spiritually change our planet forever!

Part

1

Raising Ministering Youth

PART ONE INTRODUCTION

*T*he age-old saying remains true: "The hand that rocks the cradle rules the world." The early years of home life exert powerful formative influences on our children. Many of today's youth require extensive healing from wounds inflicted in the home or from the absence of healthy parenting. Our primary goal as Christian parents must be to raise our kids in homes free of influences that tear them down and filled with influences that build them up in the Lord.

The chapters in this section highlight some of our adventures in child raising, both at home and in other significant spiritual contexts. As we parented our kids, we had no idea they would become dedicated ministers at such early ages — in their teens. Looking back, we can discern some family practices, parental attitudes, and church experiences we feel contributed to making them who they are in God. With humility we offer these to you. The last thing we want, however, is for our readers to take these concepts as an ironclad formula for producing ministering youth. Please be sensitive to the Spirit's prompting if you choose to adopt any of our suggestions. Only if He anoints them to you will our ideas bear healthy fruit in your situation. We know full well that God's grace and mercy account for any profitable parenting we have done.

1

Vision for the Joshua Generation

*E*verything begins somewhere. Ultimately, of course, this book's account of kids who grew into teen ministers began as God's idea. We believe the Lord is raising up ECA and similar youth ministries across the world because it is His intention to send forth a vast army of radical young disciples at this time in history. Through them He intends to shake and harvest the world for Jesus. We know from Scripture that what He intends to do He first announces prophetically: "Surely the Sovereign Lord does nothing without revealing His plan to His servants the prophets" (Amos 3:7). It is appropriate, therefore, that we begin by sharing a prophetic message given to Lynn when she was a teenager herself.

The Very Early Years

At age nineteen, I realized that Jesus Christ is God and invited Him to be my Savior and Lord. This was during the Jesus Movement, a move of God's Spirit that drew thousands of American countercultural youth to Christ in the early seventies. Bruce accepted the Lord at nearly the same time, when he was twenty-two. We started attending Immanuel Baptist Church in Wilmington, Delaware, where we received warm nurture and foundational discipleship from Pastor Ed Miller and many wonderful Christians.

In a short time we were given responsibility as leaders of the Jesus Movement in our city of Wilmington, Delaware. Pastor Ed, seminary-trained and every bit the professional clergyman, displayed an exceptional ability to trust us to manage our ministry as we believed God was giving it to us. This trait was God's sovereignty at work. Had this special pastor not displayed it, we could not have learned to minister as we did. We had almost complete use of the church resources — including office space, meeting areas, and counseling rooms. That generous congregation even housed a few of the brothers among us for many months in the third floor of their office building, without charge. Clearly Pastor Ed and Immanuel Church modeled for us then what we ended up doing for our own youth ministry, ECA, some twenty-five years later. Thank God for this excellent example of adults who trusted ministering youth in the early days of the Wilmington Jesus Movement. Our present was exciting and our future seemed filled with unlimited possibilities.

Within a year, however, through a series of difficulties, we left that caring church home. I was already estranged from my own family because I had married Bruce before finishing college. The good times turned rough. We were isolated from the Body of Christ, expecting our first child, living with Bruce's stepmother (who was experiencing marital difficulties), and Bruce was making a hand-to-mouth living selling vacuum cleaners door to door. Our present was dismal and our future looked bleak.

One hot afternoon in June, I was reading upstairs in our room at Bruce's parents' home. I was not feeling particularly spiritual because I was very wounded emotionally and not thinking much about God at the time. I say this to show you I was not in the most responsive mood for a visitation from the Holy Spirit.

As I was reading Leon Uris' *Exodus*, a book about the rebirth of Israel as a nation in 1948, the Holy Spirit suddenly started speaking clearly into my thoughts, almost as an audible voice: "Yours is the Moses Generation," I sensed Him saying. "You are carrying a child who is part of the Joshua Generation. It is this generation that will go into the Promised Land. Your generation will give birth to the Joshua Generation. It is your generation's responsibility to train and prepare the Joshua Generation to go into the promised land." I put my book down in amazement.

> It is your generation's responsibility to train and prepare the Joshua Generation to go into the promised land.

This event took place in 1972, long before any generation had been referred to as "the Joshua Generation." Although this was definitely a strong and memorable spiritual experience, frankly it didn't mean much to me at the time. I was nineteen years old, very pregnant, discouraged about my own family's alienation from me, and not excited at all about the next generation! I was going through enough of my own problems dealing with my new marriage and my own personal life. My present felt awful and I had no desire to think about the future.

Time passed. Bruce quit selling vacuum cleaners. Both of us enrolled at the University of Delaware in Newark, Delaware, Bruce as a graduate student in English and I as an undergraduate in the same field. From 1972 to 1978 we led informal praise and prayer meetings; first at our university apartment and then in various leased facilities as more people attended. In 1978 Bruce was ordained as a minister by Immanuel Church and commissioned by them to start a college-age mission church. We then formally founded Newark Christian Fellowship (NCF), where both of us now serve on the pastoral staff.

Years passed. The rest of our five children were born and raised in the context of the ministries of NCF. Throughout this time I didn't think at all about the prophetic word given to me in 1972. Then the mid-nineties arrived. Our church youth were starting to be released as radical, fiery disciples of Jesus. Previously shy youth started to preach, prophesy, evangelize, and do warfare against the enemy as fearless warriors of God who had purposed to take their generation for Christ. Youth would speak words that would change the spiritual atmosphere. I recognized a revival anointing settling upon them. God was clearly doing something new among them, but it felt somehow familiar. Was God starting a new move of His Spirit? Then I remembered the Lord's word to me in the summer of 1972. This was that — the fulfillment of His prophetic word. The Joshua Generation had arisen! ECA and similar youth revival ministries now emerging in the Church worldwide are being birthed by God, I believe, as part of His grand design to sweep an entire generation into the Kingdom.

> Will we be partners with youth in the worldwide harvest now coming on the earth?

The Lord is asking my generation a crucial question in this hour. Are we — adults from the Moses Generation — willing to fulfill our part of His vision for the Joshua generation? Are we willing to turn our attention away from our own concerns to what is a divinely given assignment: to nurture and train the youth in our churches so that both generations — Joshua and Moses — can go into the promised land together? Will we be partners with youth in the worldwide harvest now coming on the earth? Our church and Bruce and I have said "yes" to this question. Will you?

MY TIME OF ANGUISH

This book concerns what has unfolded among our youth since we answered that question in the affirmative. But the job hasn't always been easy, particularly for me as a mom. I'd like to share a very personal part of my journey with you and hopefully encourage you parents who may be going through similar situations.

When one of our children was fourteen, he started to go in an unhealthy direction. For the next several years, we watched him make choices that negatively affected his spiritual life. Try as we did through prayer, counseling, and various forms of discipline, we seemed to be powerless to stop his series of bad choices. I often had dreadful, graphic pictures in my mind of each of my children going over a cliff, falling to their destruction, while I stood by, helpless to rescue them.

> I often had dreadful, graphic pictures in my mind of each of my children going over a cliff, falling to their destruction, while I stood by, helpless to rescue them.

But God has been faithful. Those dire mental images did not materialize. In fact, three of my five children are currently core leaders of ECA, and my prodigal has come to know the Lord. My fifth child is only ten years of age but is already demonstrating a strong desire to serve God. The Lord did not leave me in my desperate condition but through that situation gave me two specific keys to help prepare our children to go into the Promised Land.

KEY #1: RELEASE YOUR ANGUISH TO THE LORD THROUGH INTERCESSORY PRAYER

> Like barren Hannah in the Old Testament, in my darkest moments I believed I might be fruitless in my effort to raise my children for God.

Like barren Hannah in the Old Testament, in my darkest moments I believed I might be fruitless in my effort to raise my children for God. As my son made more and more wrong choices, I grieved more and more. I was desperately fearful for him and concerned that he would set a negative standard that all my other children would follow.

In her grief, Hannah made a good decision: she decided to bring her intense sorrow to the Lord. As she did this, her praying was so unusually focused and consuming that Eli, the priest, concluded she was drunk. He changed his opinion later, though, and said to her, "Go in peace; and may the God of Israel grant your petition that you have asked of Him." She saw this as God's answer, thanked Eli, and happily returned home (1 Sam. 1:10-18). Something had shifted in the spiritual realm for Hannah. She no longer grieved in prayer before the Lord. Somehow, through her agonized praying, faith had come. She had, as the veteran prayer warriors call it, "prayed through."

It happened like that for me too. As I became more and more concerned for my son, I asked several other parents of troubled teens to fervently and diligently pray for all our kids with Bruce and me. They agreed. Things looked pretty dismal for us all at the beginning. It seemed the more we prayed, the worse our kids' situations became. Two of our group's teens ended up in prison and two became pregnant. Not an encouraging start!

On one particular night, however, as we were praying as usual, suddenly we all sensed something shift in the spiritual realm. Collectively we started to laugh and laugh, before that particular phenomenon had become commonplace. As we parents ended our many minutes of laughter, we knew something had changed. Like Hannah, without anything being different in the visible realm, we could go our way and be confident concerning the concerns of our hearts. Through months of praying, somehow we had pulled down heaven's substance of confident faith. This faith was now in our spirits as a sure promise — an unshakeable assurance of God's good work in the lives of our difficult children.

So the first key to reclaiming your kids and preparing them to be released as the Joshua Generation, is this: pray, pray, and pray some more! I don't think you have to be real eloquent at prayer (we weren't), but you do have to be committed, diligent, and fervent. You have to mean what you pray — really desire the answer, based on clear knowledge of His will from Scripture. God delights to reward those who approach Him with this kind of focus and dedication in prayer.

> The first key to reclaiming your kids and preparing them to be released as the Joshua Generation, is this: pray, pray, and pray some more!

KEY #2: RELEASE YOUR CHILDREN FULLY INTO HIS HANDS

America has the longest adolescence in the world. Unlike other cultures, we do not establish an exact age of transition when our children become adults. Many Christian parents whom I have spoken with believe that their children do not become adults until their mid-twenties. This confirms some of the research that shows that most Americans see adulthood as occurring around age twenty-five. This is quite different from the expectations of certain other times in

American history and of other present day cultures. During the agricultural age in America, youth understood that they became adults in their late teens. As boys became adults, they graduated to working with their dads on the farm or in the family business. Girls married and found purpose in their new adult roles as housewives and mothers.

In the past, religions in America also clearly marked the transition between youth and adulthood. Catholics did this through confirmation, Jews through bar and bas mitzvah events. While still conducted, these ceremonies no longer seem to be as meaningful in American culture as markers from youth into adulthood.

It seems that the closest Americans come to celebrating this transition is the high school graduation party. But this occasion is not a true transition marker because it does not bestow any more responsibility or status on the young adult. The adolescent is further confused because he or she is treated either as an adult or youth depending on the situation: driving at sixteen; voting at eighteen; drinking at twenty-one. Social psychologist Kurt Lewin has labeled the adolescent in contemporary society a "marginal" person who is trapped between childhood and adulthood.

Other countries more successfully mark a distinct transition between childhood and adulthood. Japan, for instance, holds an "Adults Day" celebration for all youth who have reached age eighteen. On this day the mayors of each Japanese city welcome these new adults into community life. This establishes a clear line of transition between adolescence and adulthood.

Because contemporary American society fails to offer this clear transition marker, entrance into adulthood for American youth is an ambiguous event. This ambiguity produces serious repercussions. Possibly the widespread generational rebellion of the sixties was partially caused by youth attempting to establish their own unique rites of passage into adulthood, the more traditional ones having become meaningless. Perhaps some of the present generation's choices — violent gangs, body piercings, drug and alcohol abuse, and experimentation with bizarre forms of spirituality — are adolescents' attempts to make their own initiation rites into adulthood. I believe Christian adults must give youth clear transition markers and better ways of celebrating their transition into adulthood.

Another obstacle in a teenager's growth into maturity is that American parents often have their kids' futures mapped out for them in meticulous detail. It is part of the American dream for children to graduate high school and college before entering the work force. This standard parental expectation may or may not be a good thing, depending on God's will for that child.

However, many of the Christian parents I have advised as a guidance counselor view their plans for their kids as non-negotiable. God's will does not really enter into the equation. Parental will is presumed to be God's will.

A further hindrance to a smooth transition from youth to adulthood is that Americans require their youth to go from one stage of life to another with little or no training. Developmental psychologists call this a high degree of discontinuity in our contemporary society. Youth are expected to graduate from high school and enter adulthood with little real-life preparation in how to be responsible in adult roles. They are also expected to know how to be mature marital partners as well as nurturing parents with little training in either area of life. In other words, life stage transitions are abrupt and confusing for American youth, with no continuity from one stage to the next.

Many other cultures manage life transitions in a more continuous way. In Samoa, for instance, older adults understand the importance of mentoring children and youth. Young children have a functional place in the society from early childhood; they are given meaningful tasks that have relevance to what they will be doing later in life. Young children take care of younger children. They also plant and harvest crops, working alongside adults to learn from an early age the expectations of adult life. Understandably, their transition into adult roles is smooth and much less stressful than for American youth.

Sadly, I don't see a pattern of life stage continuity within most churches either. Most Christian youth do not believe they have places of significant value and ministry in their churches. This must change. We adults must learn to give our youth a place within our churches, and we must give them meaningful work to do alongside adults. Once we make the paradigm shift from a discontinuous to a continuous culture within our minds and spirits, new ideas about bringing our youth into adult church roles will start to flow.

> I believe the
> Joshua
> Generation
> (X and Y)
> has a
> special call
> on them
> as an
> ENTIRE
> generation.

I believe the Joshua Generation (X and Y) has a special call on them as an entire generation. I believe many of them will not go the normative route into marriage and career. They are destined to serve the Lord in unconventional ways. Some will indeed be directed by the Lord to go to college to become business executives, doctors, etc., but many will be told just as validly by Him to become missionaries or worship leaders, Christian artists or youth pastors — perhaps without higher educational training as a prerequisite. We must not dictatorially decide God's will for our children's futures. We must give serious attention to their own heart desires and their personal sense of leading from the Holy Spirit.

We parents must completely release our plans for our children to the Lord so that His will can be done in their lives, no matter how unusual the unfolding of His will may appear to us. We must prepare this generation to follow God's destiny for them, not control their decision-making to fulfill our own needs or dreams. We must allow the Joshua Generation to be who they are meant to be, to walk out their special destiny in God in their unique way. Certainly we can and should guide and counsel them to help them discern the Lord's will in their lives. But we must be careful not to dominate them by imposing our personal expectations on their life paths. The Joshua generation in Scripture did things very differently than the Moses generation. We must be willing to come alongside this new generation and do those things necessary for their growth, without compelling them to do things our way.

> We must prepare this generation to follow God's destiny for them, not control their decision-making to fulfill our own needs or dreams.

My prodigal is now a Christian and part of our church. He is married to a lovely Christian woman who is expecting their second child. My son serves the Lord by giving witness to his faith in the context of a secular rock band. His fellow band members report that he is unbelievably stubborn and tenacious about his Christianity! God graciously heard my anguished cries.

Are we willing to cry out and intercede for the Joshua generation? Will we then be willing — as we see Christ formed in them — to give them fully to the Lord's plans even if their ways or methods don't meet our needs or go along with our plans? Are we willing to set them free to follow their call to lead their generation and others into the Promised Land of worldwide revival and harvest? Let's resolve to do our part so we can all go in together!

Please consider the "What Do You Think?" questions on the next page.

What Do You Think?

Parents

Examine your heart. Are you truly willing to pay the price for your kids to come to God?

How much influence do you think parents have in shaping their kids' spiritual destinies?

If you knew that praying every day for your kids would bring them to God, would you do it?

What stops you from doing this now?

Can you trust God to do what He needs to in the life of your child?

Have you released your children's futures fully into the Lord's hand?

Are you willing to accept God's call to career for your kids instead of your idea of His call?

Do you think you can advise your older children without controlling them?

2

God's Raw Material

The Founding Core Members of East Coast Aflame

The Joshua and Moses generations laboring as one, preparing the way of the Lord. It's a sweet vision, is it not? But simply as a vision, it will not happen. To bring it to fruition, youth and adults must intentionally give themselves to its accomplishment. We are blessed to be stewards of youth in our church who we humbly believe are vanguards in this new partnership venture between youth and adults. They chose years ago to give their lives to the Lord, and they are willing to link arms with adults in ministry.

We believe these young people are marked by a special destiny for such a time as this. They yearn to be God's army if only given the opportunity! Of course in other ways they are normal kids with normal kid problems. They are like all our children: besieged by temptations and trials, but full of enormous spiritual potential. Let's take a look at some of the ways God fashioned ECA core leadership for service to their generation.

The childhood of each ECA ministry team member shows marks of the formative influences of the Lord's sovereign grace in their lives. I believe we can discern hints of their call to ministry, and origins of the anointings within them that empower their work for Him. We can learn some of the ways of God by examining how certain experiences trained them for their destined missions.

For the scope of this book I have limited the young ministers I describe to the ECA youth leadership team who were part of the ministry's beginning. Others who joined in later are no less vital to the group's success, of course.

Those I describe are Christian Dunn, Jason Latshaw, Jonathan Latshaw, Jessica Latshaw, Nathan Palkovitz, Christine Mulrooney, and Rebekah Latshaw. When ECA began ministering to youth outside NCF, Jason was 19; Christian was 18; Jonathan, Christine and Rebekah were 17; Nathan was 16; and Jessica was 15.

CHRISTIAN: THE SAMUEL ANOINTING
"But Samuel ministered before the Lord, even as a child..."
1 Sam. 2:18

This little kid kept showing up at different services at my church. At thirteen, Christian was a likeable boy, friendly, very serious about God, intense. He would come to church with his parents, but instead of hanging out with other kids in some remote part of the building, he would participate in the service — lifting his hands in worship, listening closely to every word said, and observing carefully every move made by everyone. It was my distinct impression that he was watching everything about church very, very keenly — especially me! This young teen was soaking in every aspect of what happened as the Holy Spirit moved through specific types of services at our church.

Later I learned that Christian had been born somewhat miraculously, in a medical sense. Diagnosed with chronic lupus, his mother was told by doctors that she could not conceive and give birth. Yet by grace she did, and she named her son Christian as a testimony to God's merciful intervention.

In school Christian was popular with his teachers and peers, though he received some mild persecution for being too "good" a Christian (rather ironic at an evangelical Christian school). He played soccer and basketball and was a class leader and a straight-A student. It was clear to all who came to know him that in addition to possessing strong natural talents, Christian was, spiritually, an exceptionally compelled young man. I had the distinct sense he was somehow being prepared for something week after week, month after month, year after year.

One evening at church, the Spirit came in power as we worshipped. An unusually intense prophetic anointing electrified the room. Suddenly I found myself laying hands on Christian and uttering a flow of prophetic words over his life. I could see that he was truly called of the Lord — a call to dedicated ministry, to a life of service and power in the Lord. His current problems, fears, self-doubts, and hesitations would all be swept away by the sanctifying hand of the Lord as he

> His pastor's heart, prophetic exhortations, and strong leadership abilities give ample evidence to the fulfillment of the Samuel anointing on Christian's life.

grew in favor with God and man. I knew then that Christian had a special leadership destiny in God.

All our destinies in Him are special of course, yet not many experience that Samuel call to be separated to purity and ministry unto the Lord even from our youth. Not many are conceived as an answer to prayer from a barren mother.

Christian's fervent spirit and genuine love for God and people manifest themselves in his powerful and distinctive style of drumming. His percussion drives the dynamism of the ECA worship team. His pastor's heart, prophetic exhortations, and strong leadership abilities give ample evidence to the fulfillment of the Samuel anointing on Christian's life.

JASON: THE DANIEL ANOINTING

"...young men in whom there was no blemish...gifted in all wisdom, possessing knowledge and quick to understand, who had the ability to serve in the king's palace..."
Dan. 1:4

Jason was a different sort of little boy. Unlike many of his peers, worldly things held virtually no attraction for him. From an early age he and his two younger siblings felt very little desire to pursue satisfactions and pleasures outside the boundaries of God's loving law. Jason was repulsed by what many call "normal" experiments with sin and the interpersonal peer conflicts of childhood and adolescence. We noticed that even as a young teen, Jason was sought out by his siblings and many of his peers for his counsel to help them solve personal and life problems. He seemed to possess a gift of wisdom from an early age.

Jason displayed ability to learn quickly and do nearly anything in life he set his hand to. (With the exception of getting his driver's license at age sixteen — but we won't examine this ugly blemish on Jason's otherwise spotless record of accomplishments.) He was a star achiever in virtually every area of academic life, an athlete, a musician, an artist, and a leader in his class and among his many friends. He absorbed the realities of Christianity as enthusiastically and easily as he drank in the rest of life.

Lynn and I spent many hours of prayer dedicating our gifted son to the Lord, asking Him for a consistent outpouring of grace into this boy's spirit, soul, and body. Specifically our prayer was that Jason's many gifts would be used by the Lord for His glory and for the extension of His Kingdom.

We believed our primary job with this young man was to present him with as many contexts for the expression and growth of His gifts as we could. We offered him lessons in music and art, enrolled him in basketball leagues, and encouraged him to take part in a summer program for young scholars in Washington, D.C. A youth of recognized honors and achievements, Jason most importantly grew as well in his knowledge of Scripture, his love of God, and his zeal to serve Him with excellence. He grew in favor with God and man. A model of "success" by any standard, Jason's heart burns to see Christian ministry expressed through the same kind of excellence and quality he is accustomed to seeing in all that he does personally.

When he teaches, he expounds the Scriptures with the thoroughness and care of the scholar. When he creates songs for the ECA worship team, he marries depth of lyric with excellence of sound. And when he writes original biblically

> A model of "success" by any standard, Jason's heart burns to see Christian ministry expressed through the same kind of excellence and quality he is accustomed to seeing in all that he does personally.

based dramas, he does so with quality and a righteous professionalism far beyond his years.

By God's grace, Jason is a young adult whose "manner of life from [his] youth up", like Paul's in Acts 26:4 and Daniel's in the court of Nebuchadnezzar, stands up well under close scrutiny. The Daniel anointing is often strongly evident on those whom the Lord gifts to serve Him with royal excellence. Jason has been given that anointing.

JONATHAN: THE GIDEON ANOINTING

"So Gideon said to Him, 'O my Lord, how can I save Israel? Indeed my clan is the weakest in Manasseh, and I am the least in my father's house." Judg. 6:15

Jason's younger brother by two years, Jonathan was a smallish, skinny kid with big fears. As confident and filled with an easy self-esteem as was Jason, Jonathan was just the opposite. Early in Christian school, Jonathan fell to the lower half of his class in reading and didn't thrive scholastically like Jason did. We remember him often returning home from school frustrated and anxious. For Jonathan's emotional and spiritual well-being, we made the then-difficult decision to withdraw him from school and teach him at home. This decision proved wise.

Jonathan's personal growth as an effective Christian has hinged on overcoming a seemingly endless series of challenges because of his one enormous and ever-present problem: fear. He feared looking different and not blending in with his peers. He was afraid of the dark and of sleeping alone in his own bedroom. Both Jonathan and his sister Jessica spent many nights able to sleep only in the safe environment of our bedroom. Jonathan was painfully shy, would never speak in public, and was afraid of failure.

Of our three boys, Jonathan was the physically weakest and most fearful. (He has reminded me to write that, in fairness, he was also a fearsome competitor in sports, particularly basketball and football, where it seems his fears had no hold on him whatsoever!)

I recall two incidents that seem pivotal in Jonathan's deliverance from his besetting fears. One night, Jonathan, Jessica, and I found ourselves in a very intense conversation about something those two greatly feared: demons. Our church teaches the reality of the demonic, and we train our people to conduct successful spiritual warfare against demons. Somehow this dimension of spiritual life had become real to these two kids, and they were quite curious — and afraid (of course) — about it. Their young minds (they were perhaps eight- and ten-years-old at the time) moved quickly from question to question about the demonic world and the interaction between Christians and demons. "How can demons attack us? Can they get to us in our house? Can they read our minds? What do we do if they come after us? How can we know if they are coming after us?"

This line of questioning gave me a wonderful window of opportunity to teach them about the authority Christians have in Christ over all demonic activity: "Behold, I have given you authority and power to tread on snakes and scorpions and over the power of the enemy, and nothing shall injure you" (Luke 10:19).

I explained how the Lord's authority is accessed and used by believers, and what we can expect the results to be. I shared that fear is one of the demons' prime weapons against us, and that, in fact, fear is often not just the result of a demon's attack. Often, I explained, the feeling of fear emanates from the demon of fear itself

> Jonathan's personal growth as an effective Christian has hinged on overcoming a seemingly endless series of challenges because of his one enormous and ever-present problem: FEAR.

> Jonathan and Jessica saw that through the name of Jesus, Christians could push back the attack of spiritual enemies like fear, doubt, and failure in order to obey God's directives in their lives.

in its attempt to paralyze us hinder us from doing God's will. I instructed Jonathan and Jessica in how to resist the enemy personally, out loud, then showed them in Scripture that when they did this, they could expect demons to flee: "Resist the devil, and he will flee from you" (James 4:7).

Suddenly the light of God's truth broke into their spirits. Jonathan and Jessica saw that through the name of Jesus, Christians could push back the attack of spiritual enemies like fear, doubt, and failure in order to obey God's directives in their lives. The word of God's truth in Scripture was beginning to empower them in their spirits and souls.

This word of new truth was soon to be tested through the second incident I remember about Jonathan and his fears. Up to this time, Jonathan had slept nearly every night of his life either upstairs in our bedroom or next door in his sister's bedroom. Bedroom floors were simply huge beds to him. Lynn had successfully helped our son overcome many fear-related difficulties in the past. She and I decided it was now time for Jonathan to tackle perhaps the fiercest of his fear giants. We informed him we believed it was time for him to begin to sleep all night in his own room, in his own bed.

As you can guess, this prospect absolutely petrified Jonathan. But a slowly growing trust in and courage from the Lord was preparing him to confront this new challenge. As bedtime arrived, Jonathan, with choked-up voice and moist eyes, parked his blanket and pillow in the doorway of the room — nowhere near his bed, but indeed, in his own room! He slept barely a wink but did manage to survive spending the entire night in his own room. And from that time on, Jonathan, his fear overcome, slept in his bedroom night after night. God is good.

As Jonathan reentered his Christian high school after several years of homeschooling, the Lord gave him additional training in overcoming the twin terror giants of singing and speaking in public — two actions which have turned out to be vital components of his ministry call. At age sixteen, Jonathan decided to try for a core role in his school's annual musical production. His old enemy, fear, gripped him as the time came for his audition, but by grace Jonathan pushed through this panic and squeezed out a song well enough to get the part. In his junior and senior years, when faced with presenting oral reports, Jonathan's face would turn bright red as he started to speak. But in this too the Lord gave him an overcoming spirit. The promises of God in Isa. 54:4 & 14 proved true in his life:

> "Fear not, for you will not be put to
> shame; neither feel humiliated, for you
> will not be disgraced; but you will forget
> the shame of your youth... In
> righteousness you will be established;
> you will be far from oppression, for you
> will not fear..."

On commencement day, the Lord's ability to turn failure into success was highlighted as Jonathan graduated from high school with honors.

Once a "timid Timothy," Jonathan has become the prophetic warrior/leader of the ECA worship team, now called "gate called Beautiful." His leadership strength persistently pulverizes the gates of hell until Heaven's objectives are met through pounding praise and intimate worship of the Lord. His Gideon anointing compels him not only to a radical

> Jonathan's leadership strength persistently pulverizes the gates of hell until Heaven's objectives are met through pounding praise and intimate worship of the Lord.

boldness of worship leading but produces a powerful preaching style that grips the hearts of those who hear and draws them to repentance and uncompromising commitment to Jesus. Jonathan possesses the revivalist's anointing.

In weakness and honesty Jonathan first approached the Lord like a timid young Jeremiah "...'Alas, Lord God! Behold, I do not know how to speak, because I am a youth.'" And as the Lord strengthened the anxious prophet for his mission, so a similar encouragement now compels Jonathan: "Do not be afraid of them, for I am with you to deliver you...Behold, I have put My words in your mouth" (Jer. 1:6-9). His journey from paralyzing shyness to courageous overcoming is testimony to God's not having given Jonathan "a spirit of fear, but of power and love and a sound mind" (2 Tim. 1:7).

JESSICA: THE DEBORAH ANOINTING

"I will sing to the Lord, I will sing; I will make music to the Lord, the God of Israel."
Judg. 5:3

Jessica — Jason and Jonathan's younger sister — was quite similar to Jonathan in many ways. In age nineteen months apart, they were so nearly inseparable as youngsters that Lynn and I called them our twins. Jessica's natural personality mirrored Jonathan's. She too was excruciatingly shy, preferring to observe situations passively from a distance, terrified of jumping into the middle of things. She would, quite literally, hide behind Lynn and peek out at life from that place of insulated safety. We wondered (and prayed much about) whether Jessica and Jonathan — two very special but extraordinarily fearful kids — could ever make their way in the "real world," let alone do anything significant in God's Kingdom.

Jessica hated to be viewed as imperfect. To be corrected or rebuked reduced her to tears, so she worked very hard to achieve perfection in all areas. At home she tried to be perfectly obedient to the wishes of her parents (which was very nice for us of course!). At school she was so nearly perfect that at evaluation time her first grade teacher remarked that she was ... well ... "perfect" and didn't need improvement in anything.

But she was as painfully quiet and shy among most of her classmates as she was in public. The inevitable schoolyard taunting and competitiveness took their toll on Jessica's sensitive nature. Eventually, despite an excellent academic record at school, she too chose to be home schooled along with her brother Jonathan.

One potential difficulty with homeschooled kids is social and "real world" isolation. Therefore Lynn and I decided Jessica needed to become involved in at least one sport. She could choose from three — swimming, horseback riding, or dancing. Fearful of all three of course, but forced by us to make a choice, she reluctantly chose to begin dance lessons at age eight. Her dance training has continued, and Jessica embraced the values of self-discipline, hard work, and personal productivity through it.

Then, suddenly, years after she started dancing, Jessica began to sing. This was a very odd thing to us at the time, because before then we had heard her hum, even perhaps sing almost inaudibly as many young kids do when in groups. She had had a small solo part in a kindergarten play. Lynn and

> Jessica too was excruciatingly shy, preferring to observe situations passively from a distance, terrified of jumping into the middle of things.

> Jessica's early exposure to dance, song, and the piano would providentially prepare her to play a leading role in creating the kind of unique prophetic art and music ECA is bringing forth to impact their generation for the Lord.

I thought she appeared to have a decent voice but certainly nothing earthshaking.

But abruptly, one evening in the family car, Jessica started to sing! I mean really sing. Music from the Broadway production of *Les Miserables* was playing through our car's cassette player. Several family members were singing along. Quite unexpectedly this strong, sweet female voice soared into auditory prominence. It was quiet little Jessica, suddenly singing! She hasn't stopped.

Piano lessons followed, along with the constant dance training. Then came the composition of Jessica's first worship song, "In You", which opened a floodgate of original music from a girl formerly so shy she would never say — not to mention sing — a word in public. Little did any of us suspect that Jessica's early exposure to dance, song, and the piano would providentially prepare her to play a leading role in creating the kind of unique prophetic art and music ECA is bringing forth to impact their generation for the Lord.

Like the prophetess Deborah, Jessica possesses an anointing to lead many in the Kingdom through wisdom, strength of character, and gifts of musical artistry. Her talents in songwriting, choreography, preaching, and bold prophetic singing illustrate God's delight to bring forth His glory in diversely creative ways. We believe the Lord has released Jessica's many artistic abilities through His Spirit as her singular psalmistry presents Jesus to her peers among the Joshua generation.

NATHAN: THE JAMES ANOINTING

"Who is wise and understanding among you? Let him show it by his good life, by deeds done in humility that comes from wisdom." James 3:13

Tall and physically strong, Nathan might be aptly described as a pillar of the ECA ministry team. The first son among four brothers, Nathan was nurtured in a close, loving Christian family environment. Family getaways to remote campgrounds and wilderness areas consumed many of his weekends and prepared Nathan to serve others with diligence, responsibility, and wisdom.

Disciplined and studious, Nathan manifests a practical obedience to the commands of God and a thorough knowledge of Scripture. His caring pastor's heart carries an unwavering commitment to see the hearts of youth turn to the Lord and avoid the pitfalls of sin.

Nathan's teachings at ECA meetings are practical biblical exhortations for his peers to stay devoted to the Lord, obedient to His Word, and committed to the brethren. The James pastoral anointing flows through Nathan's life of wise counsel and humble service to many.

> Nathan's teachings at ECA meetings are practical biblical exhortations for his peers to stay devoted to the Lord, obedient to His Word, and committed to the brethren.

CHRISTINE: THE JAEL ANOINTING

"Most blessed of women be Jael....Her hand reached for the tent peg, her right hand for the workman's hammer. She struck Sisera, she crushed his head." Judg. 5:24-26

Now the Jael anointing might not seem, at first, to be a flattering description of Christine or of any woman. Little is known about Jael from Scripture. But she is obviously

Through distinct words and warfare dance, the Jael anointing empowers Christine to proclaim Christ and be an example to young women of her generation.

a heroic biblical figure of such stature that the Spirit saw fit to record permanent praise of her exploits in Deborah's song of victory in Judges 4. There we see that Jael was a warrior woman, a fighter for God. She crushed the head of her enemy in the physical realm even as we are called to participate with Jesus in the spiritual crushing of the head of our enemy, Satan: "And the God of peace will soon [quickly] crush Satan under your feet" (Rom. 16:20).

Like Jael, Christine is a fearless spiritual warrior. Her tent peg and hammer of choice are powerful proclamations of God's Word and strong, anointed warfare dance. With these weapons of praise, she crushes demonic opposition in the spiritual atmosphere and helps open the door of worship so crucial to the flow of revival anointing at ECA conferences.

A stutterer as a child, Christine endured painful teasing at school because of this difficulty, her personal purity, and her uncompromising stand for Jesus. Now the Lord has turned this former stutterer into a passionate preacher, boldly calling her generation to repentance and holy relationship with Jesus, the Lover of her soul. As Isa. 32:4 promises to those strengthened by the Messiah: "And the tongue of the stammerers will hasten to speak clearly." Through distinct words and warfare dance, the Jael anointing empowers Christine to proclaim Christ and be an example to young women of her generation.

REBEKAH: THE HANNAH ANOINTING

"Sing, O barren women, you who never born a child; burst into song, shout for joy...says the Lord." Isa. 54:1

"In bitterness of soul Hannah wept much and prayed to the Lord." 1 Sam. 1:10

Rebekah, married to Jonathan, was single when she joined the ECA worship and ministry teams. Because of her parents' divorce, she was shuttled back and forth from one house to another during much of her childhood with no permanent place to call home. Disappointed and confused by relationship failures and personal problems, Rebekah needed substantial healing after recommitting her life to Jesus at age seventeen.

Quite gifted in verbal expression, music, and drama, Rebekah, as a child, had experienced church only in the context of strict prohibition against instrumental music and women in authoritative ministries. She wondered if there was a place in church for her artistic and speaking abilities. She wanted to express them for Christ but found no opportunity. Having known church in no other context, Rebekah remembers finding it strange and disconcerting that one day, at age twelve, in a kind of daydream, she imagined herself standing before her church congregation, preaching from her heart against apathy and passionless Christianity. Little did she suspect then that this was a prophetic

> Rebekah's own healing from personal difficulties and emotional wounds has prepared her to minister the Lord's healing to the broken-hearted, (Isa. 61:1) the severely wounded among today's youth.

33 𝓑

foreshadowing of the kind of impassioned, dramatic preaching she was destined to do to reach her generation for Christ. Her times of Hannah-like sorrow and intercession for her spiritually barren generation fuel a fiery message of hope and healing. Her own healing from personal difficulties and emotional wounds has prepared her to minister the Lord's healing to the brokenhearted, (Isa. 61:1) the severely wounded among today's youth.

Rebekah's powerful voice adds resonance and prophetic creativity to the ECA worship team. Her exhortations during worship lift all participants to a place of intimate devotion to the Lord and liberty in His presence. Her songwriting skills are emerging, and she often adds dramatic flair to her skillful presentation of the Word. The Hannah anointing in Rebekah is giving birth to lasting fruit in the Kingdom, particularly among the young women of her generation.

ONLY BY GRACE

"By the grace of God I am what I am," proclaimed the apostle Paul. It would be foolishness not to give full credit to the sovereign purpose of God for the gifts and ministries that propel the destinies of the founding core members of ECA. He has been truly faithful! And these young ministers have done their part by being radically obedient to follow the Lord wherever His Spirit has led them.

What Do You Think?

Youth & Adults

As you look at yourself (if a young person) or your kids (if a parent), do you see personality flaws only or do you see opportunities for God to show His wisdom and power through human weakness? What particular strengths do you think God could make from the specific weaknesses you see?

Youth

Do you feel you are like any of the kids described in this chapter? Which ones? Why?

Parents

Can you identify the beginning of certain kinds of spiritual gifts in your kids? Those undeveloped gifts are God's spiritual raw material. How do you think you can start to shape that raw material in Kingdom directions as God leads?

Structuring Family

3

To Produce On-Fire Kids

By God's grace, ECA's ministry team consists of exemplary Christian young people. Each of their lives shows the outworking of God's redemption and creative activity in their personalities and life experiences. Of course they have their flaws (just ask their parents!), but they are distinctively Christ-like in many ways that, frankly, put us older folks to a certain amount of shame by comparison. Sure, they haven't had to overcome the consequences of the kinds of sinful decisions their parents made in their own teen years; but they had the opportunity to make sinful decisions, and for the most part they did not make them. I believe God has guarded and shepherded their decisions especially for His own purposes.

We are often asked as parents and church leaders what we did to cause these kids to love and serve God with such devotion and passion. When we were first asked this question, we were stumped; honestly we hadn't considered that we had anything to do with it! In this chapter I try to provide an answer.

GOD'S SOVEREIGN GRACE

Lynn and I know we've made numerous mistakes raising our children, so it's not at all difficult for us to be humble as we try to tell others what we did to raise up our ministering kids. All credit really does belong to the Lord. We know that who they are in God and what they will do for Him ultimately has everything to do with His sovereign call and destiny for their lives. Maybe we should write a book on the child-rearing mistakes we've made! But since we are frequently asked child-rearing questions, I have tried to identify a few keys we've discovered that seem to have drawn our kids to God.

> Maybe we should write a book on the child-rearing mistakes we've made!

HANNAH/SAMUEL:
A PICTURE OF RAISING MINISTERING YOUTH

Hannah's method for raising her destined-to-minister son provides an instructive parallel to how we raised ours. In 1 Samuel 1 we observe Hannah engaged in four distinct child-rearing processes or events as she shepherded her son into the service of the Lord:

- she prayed for Samuel;
- she nursed Samuel;
- she weaned Samuel; and
- she dedicated Samuel.

Prayer

First, the circumstances of Samuel's birth and future in God were overwhelmingly bathed in prayer by Hannah:

> "And she, greatly distressed, prayed to
> the Lord and wept bitterly. And she
> made a vow... Now it came about, as
> she continued praying before the
> Lord... For this boy I prayed, and the
> Lord has given me my petition which I
> asked of Him" (1 Sam. 1:10-12; 27).

Note here the primacy, the passion, the purposefulness, and the persistence of Hannah's prayer work.

Facing the shame of childlessness, the primary impulse of Hannah's soul was toward God in prayer. She converted the pain of her heart's anguish into passionate petitioning of the Lord. Her purposefulness to obtain God's provision was so unswerving and solemn that she made a vow to the Lord—not a light thing in a religious culture where vow making was regarded with the utmost seriousness (Deut. 23:21). Not content to approach Him just once, Hannah continued praying until assurance of the answer was hers. This praying mom's example should inspire all Christian parents to press in to God through prayer until we see our youth wholly Christ's in every way.

Nursing

The second feature of Hannah's raising Samuel for God is nursing her son. Let's view this nursing process as more than the biological flow of nurturing substance from parent to child. I believe it is a picture of the flow of spiritual substance as well. Physically, nursing is the transmission of food from a mother into her offspring for the purpose of imparting *bios* (the Greek for "physical/natural life"). But as we raise youth ministers, we must supply them *eith* spiritual nursing, which I see as the transfer of *zoe* (Greek for "spiritual life") from parent to child. As Hannah nursed Samuel, I can imagine her sharing the story of the torment of her barrenness, her journey of faith and desperation for God to supply her need, and the miracle of her son's birth. I can hear her singing songs of praise and adoration as her child drew life from her body.

Paul played this role with his spiritual offspring at Thessalonica:

> "But we proved to be gentle among you,
> as a nursing mother tenderly cares for
> her own children" (1 Thess. 2:7).

We parents must spiritually nurse our children. We must consciously and regularly pour into them the truths we have learned from God, the methods we use to approach Him, the stories of our encounters with Him, and the practical ways we walk out our life by His grace. If we do this, the realities of Christ we have received in our lives will be absorbed as spiritual substance by our offspring and help form Christ in them. We parents must deliberately form spiritual bonds with our children, imparting Christ within us through open communication and heart-to-heart intimacy. This will provide a solid foundation on which the Holy Spirit may build the things of Christ unique to their own lives and ministries. This will enable them to go far beyond what we have done in the Lord. It will help make their calling sure.

> We parents must spiritually nurse our children.

Weaning

Literally, weaning is the training of a child to obtain food in ways other than nursing. It implies that the child lets go of the total dependence on a nurturing adult that nursing

> To wean a child spiritually means, in my view, to permit your child a growing freedom to make wise, age-appropriate choices in all areas of life.

provides. For parents, weaning implies a voluntary abandonment of primary provision-giving — a letting go of what has been to that point righteous and needed control over a child in order to sustain that child's life. The mother must shut down that easy and natural way of provision her child has grown accustomed to so that her child can learn new eating skills. Weaning is a crucial and necessary developmental step for a child, the first step toward independence. To wean a child spiritually means, in my view, to permit your child a growing freedom to make wise, age-appropriate choices in all areas of life. A young person must have structured opportunities to learn to make individual decisions for which he/she is held accountable. This is vital to a young minister's ability to accept and effectively discharge future ministry responsibilities.

Dedication
Her prayer work done, her son nursed to an appropriate age and weaned, Hannah undertakes the final event in empowering her son to minister: she releases control of his future by giving his life into the hand of the Lord. She does this through the solemn act of dedication:

> "So I have also dedicated him to the Lord;
> as long as he lives he is dedicated to the
> Lord" (1 Sam. 1:28).

Note that this act of dedication is not temporary but permanent, lasting "as long as he lives." Parents of ministering youth must prepare to relinquish all personal, vocational, and marital dreams we have for our kids. (This may include our own unfulfilled career/marriage dreams as well.) We must unequivocally abandon all unrighteous control and manipulation of the life paths of our ministering youth. Just as Hannah let go and dedicated Samuel to the Lord and His service, so we must do as our youth enter the ministries appointed and anointed by the Lord for their lives.

> We must unequivocally abandon all unrighteous control and manipulation of the life paths of our ministering youth.

THE PRIMACY OF PRAYER

> First and certainly foremost, from the time the first of our five children was born, we prayed God's grace into their lives on a daily basis.

Looking back over our child raising years, I see that the key features of Hannah's raising of Samuel — prayer, nursing, weaning, and dedication — were manifested in what we did with our kids as well, in very imperfect ways of course.

First and certainly foremost, from the time the first of our five children was born, we prayed God's grace into their lives on a daily basis. In my opinion this is by far the most important factor that produced their growth in the Lord. I can remember the specifics of my nightly intercession for our kids. "Lord," I would pray, "pour Your grace into (child's name)'s spirit, soul, and body. Bring forth his/her natural and spiritual gifts and use them all to advance Your Kingdom!" That's basically it. Nothing fancy or long. I

> We knew our own parenting skills were so inadequate that we truly needed to pray... a lot!

seldom varied these words, although we prayed for other concerns specific to each child as well. We knew our own parenting skills were so inadequate that we truly needed to pray...a lot!

Now I know I make a lot of mistakes, but one thing I can do well is to keep on doing something. I am gifted with dogged persistence. By God's grace that's a trait I believe can be positive in my personality (of course it can be negative as well, but that's another book — confessional literature), and I believe that the Lord has used it to generate fruit through prayer for our kids.

Recall the parable Jesus told about the man who came to another man asking for bread for his friend (Luke 11:5-10). Do you remember the surprising reason Jesus gave to explain why the man who needed bread obtained what he asked for? He said simply, "...because of his persistence" (Luke 11:8). Not because of the magnitude of his faith, or his impressive words, or even because of his friendship with the bread-supplier. His need was met simply because he kept asking, seeking, and knocking — over and over and over — and he did not stop asking until he received the desired result. It seems that a divinely motivated stubbornness was at work here.

> I am eternally relieved and delighted that God is considerably more faithful than we are, aren't you?

Block-headed stubbornness being my strong suit, I prayed basically the same thing, unwaveringly, for each one of my kids nearly every day, literally for years — prayers uncreative, obligatory, drab, even boring. Sometimes Lynn and I prayed together. But more often we prayed individually. Probably had we prayed as a couple more often for our kids, more grace would have come to them. I am eternally relieved and delighted that God is considerably more faithful than we are, aren't you? We firmly believe that persistent, heartfelt prayer over many years was the most important thing we did for our kids to develop them into on-fire ministering youth. And you can do this too. It may take many years to see the answers, so start now. And, as proclaimed by that stubborn hero of wartime Britain, Winston Churchill: "Never, never, never give up."

WALKING THE WALK IN FRONT OF THEM

A second key that I believe helped ignite our kids for the Lord was that we lived our Christianity in front of them. We did not hide from their view the realities of our faith. In particular we were very open about the practical aspects of our walk in Him. Our kids saw and heard us pray and worship openly at home, so at a young age they developed informal conversational prayer to the Lord themselves and joined in church, clapping and dancing with joy in the Lord.

At home they observed us meditating on and studying the Bible and feeding on books on the Christian life. They heard us discuss issues of modern culture as they related to our faith. We told them about our lives as non-Christians and what was unhealthy and destructive about our sinful behaviors. They saw the distinct difference in our family life between times covered by prayer and times when we failed to intentionally invite the Lord into

> A second key that I believe helped ignite our kids for the Lord was that we lived our Christianity in front of them. We did not hide from their view the realities of our faith.

> Because
> Christianity
> was true
> for us,
> it rang
> as true
> for them
> as well,
> and as
> they grew
> they made
> our faith
> their own.

our circumstances. They therefore experienced firsthand the difference the presence of the Lord makes in daily events; they learned that things really do go better with God.

When we sinned against them in word or deed, we went to them, confessed our faults, and asked their forgiveness, which they learned to give. They then learned to do the same with one another and with their peers. They also witnessed conflict and reconciliation in our marriage.

We talked informally about the ways God was working in our lives, and we openly thanked Him when He provided for us and answered our prayers. We didn't hide spiritual warfare realities from them, as if somehow kids cannot defeat demons in Jesus' Name. When fear was in the house and we'd all awaken from tormenting nightmares, we'd demonstrate our authority over demons in Jesus' Name, and the peace of God would return in our home. They learned to do the same. We weren't private about our faith. We openly showed them our struggles and victories in the Lord. Therefore, because Christianity was true for us, it rang as true for them as well, and as they grew they made our faith their own.

Help Them Find Their Gifts

The third key is that we helped our children discover and develop their gifts. We believe each one of our children possesses unique gifts from the Lord in both natural and spiritual realms. Therefore we believe it is our parental responsibility to provide structured occasions for them to experiment with and grow in their God-given gifts. Lynn was excellent at inculcating these truths in our kids. Because of this, each one knew he or she had the God-given capacity to do at least one significant thing with success and excellence.

Sometimes we wish it wasn't the case, but Lynn and I are not strong in math or science. We're more arts-oriented people, and we seem to have reproduced offspring after our kind. We were hoping that at least one of our kids would have a predominant math / administrative / organizational / business gifting (somebody's got to make some money to support the rest of us!), but it didn't happen. (It must be said in fairness, however [at Jason's humble suggestion], that Jason's gifts do in fact include superior math and logical thinking abilities.)

But God has used the natural "right brain" gifts of our kids to sharpen spiritual capacities in them that are destined, in my view, to impact their generation in ways today's youth are wired to understand and find attractive. Spirit-infused creativity — in musical, visual, and dramatic expressions — has generated a compelling, appealing, and anointed presentation of the gospel of Jesus Christ through ECA. Our job as parents is to help our kids identify the strengths of their particular personalities and then provide ample opportunity for them to develop these strengths into powerful ministry tools in the hand of the Lord.

> Our job as parents is to help our kids identify the strengths of their particular personalities and then provide ample opportunity for them to develop these strengths into powerful ministry tools in the hand of the Lord.

HELP THEM GROW IN MAKING DECISIONS

We had learned to trust them in natural things, so it was logical to trust them in spiritual things.

A fourth key involved granting our kids increasing decision-making freedom to the extent that they earned it by proving responsible in lesser things. Of course it is a biblical principle that "he who proves faithful in small things will be entrusted with greater things" (Luke 16:10). We found this to be very important in equipping our kids to take meaningful spiritual responsibility in ministry at a relatively early age.

For example, each of our kids was expected to do his or her own wash at age twelve. If they wanted clean clothes, they became responsible for washing and drying their clothes. Rewards and privileges were tied to faithful accomplishment of chores and other responsibilities. When curfews became relevant to their lives, they retained the privilege of going out with their friends to the extent that they obeyed the imposed curfew. This accountability structure is a basic truth about building a sense of responsibility into a child's life. We certainly were not perfect in applying this truth, but we managed to accomplish the basics. Our children acquired skills to lead and minister in spiritual things because they had first learned to be responsible decision-makers in natural things. We had learned to trust them in natural things, so it was logical to trust them in spiritual things.

RAISE THEM IN A YOUTH-FRIENDLY CHURCH

The fifth key is raising kids in a "kid-friendly" church. That topic is covered in detail in chapter 13. Suffice it to say here that involving our kids in the youth-friendly atmosphere of our church was crucial to nurturing and releasing our kids into spiritual participation and ministry.

WHAT ABOUT DISCIPLINE?

We disciplined our kids for undesirable attitudes and behaviors through controlled spanking and other forms of negative consequences. And like most Christian parents, over time we adopted various formulas for disciplining our children, each with varying degrees of success.

We did not, however, punish our kids in the context of the development of their relationship with God. We did require that they go to church regularly and participate in the church's activities for kids. We certainly suggested that they develop foundational Christian disciplines like regular Bible reading and prayer. But we did not compel them to believe exactly as we did or worship, pray, and have devotions precisely according to our preferences.

For a time, one of our sons was not particularly comfortable with certain spiritual gifts and the worship practices normative in charismatic churches. So we were careful not to pressure him and let him work it out for himself. Jason worked through these issues and is now at peace with his own and our church's forms of worship.

As questions arose in our kids' minds we tried to honestly explain the biblical basis for what we did in Christ as persons, as a family, and as a church. We also let them know that other Christians understood these matters differently, and why. But we did not discipline them to pray, worship, read Scripture, or witness according to our specifications. We prayed for them; lived out our walk openly; and counseled, encouraged, and made suggestions to them. We did not discipline their spirituality.

> Because we never compelled our children to attach themselves to our precise form of faith, they did not have to detach themselves from it.

In retrospect I believe this was important because it granted our kids freedom to choose how they would relate to Jesus on their own. It eliminated the need many Christian kids feel to break away from the Christianity of their parents. Because we never compelled our children to attach themselves to our precise form of faith, they did not have to detach themselves from it. They developed their own individually chosen, living relationships with God relatively early in their lives.

A Family Life in Grace and Mercy

If you exit this chapter with the sense that Lynn and I have unearthed the secrets of successful Christian child-rearing and are imparting them from the mountaintop to you hapless parental misfits, then I have utterly failed to communicate the actual truth! If we consistently did anything effective year in and year out, I would say that we really did pray. So I want to exhort you: prayer is effective. When you pray faithfully for your kids, God's transforming love will cover your parenting mistakes. As you pray, He will reveal specific child-raising strategies that will be effective in your particular family. He is faithful to us even when we miserably fail Him! As you pray, His grace will prevail.

What Do You Think?

Adults

What is the one thing Bruce and Lynn did that they felt was truly effective in raising their kids for God?

How can you improve this discipline in your life?

Is there a specific prayer commitment you feel God is calling you to make for your kids?

What specific prayer targets do you feel He has set before you in relation to your kids?

Do you make it a point to live your Christianity openly in front of your kids? What could you do practically to walk this out more effectively?

Are there ways you might be wrongfully disciplining your kids in spiritual things?

Without compromising scriptural standards of morality and behavior, do you think you are extending sufficient freedom for your kids to find their own approach to the Lord? If not, how could you begin doing that?

Have you tried to identify areas of giftedness in your children? Have you provided opportunities for the development of those gifts? If not, jot down some ways you could do that now.

Do you demonstrate an overly protective, "smother love" toward your children? Do you do everything for them and make decisions on their behalf?

Consider what kinds of decisions they could begin making now that will give them experience and growth in decision making.

Casual Mentoring

4

An Alternative to Regular Family Devotions

We feel thoroughly ill-equipped giving counsel to others on how to structure family life to produce kids who love and serve God. It's certainly fair to say we fell far below the mark in being excellent parents. This chapter shows you just one area of our failure and showcases God's remarkable ability to display His redemptive power in the context of pervasive human weakness and failure.

WE BLEW IT!

For years the Latshaw family attempted regular family devotions. The problem was, they absolutely did not work for us. Not for lack of trying, certainly — we persevered week in, week out, for years — but they simply didn't work. Perhaps this was because all in our family were by nature more artistically oriented and preferred an atmosphere of unstructured, fluid interactions — which did not appear to be anything like what we understood family devotions to be. Or maybe we failed because we just didn't operationalize the program correctly. Whatever the reasons, our weekly family devotions were miserable experiences for all concerned.

> Our weekly family devotions were miserable experiences for all concerned.

Jason would like you to know that he wishes he could comment on these devotions, but he was unfortunately asleep at the time, as were all the Latshaw children.

Many successful ministers of God are shaped as children in an arena of highly disciplined spiritual training and regular family devotions. Susanna Wesley, for instance, produced two sons, John and Charles, whose accomplishments for God transformed the Western Church through a revival known as the First Great Awakening. It is well known that Susanna inculcated in all her children standards of discipline and methodical obedience to God that caused young John Wesley's brand of Christianity to be appropriately labeled "Methodism." Obviously the fruit of Susanna's regular family devotions was superb.

But our fruit was foul indeed. Every child in the family dreaded family devotions. Some other way, we knew, had to be found if we were going to be able to transmit Christ to our children.

CASUAL MENTORING

> We found that their receptivity to learning the things of God could not be commanded by us.

Probably by default, therefore, we developed what might be termed *casual mentoring* as the most effective method for training our children in the things of God. We discovered that our kids were not always receptive to the carefully selected spiritual truths we had prepared to impart to them during family devotions. They felt they had learned most of it in church and Christian school contexts. We found that their receptivity to learning the things of God could not be commanded by us. But there were times, particularly in the context of real-life experience, when their spirits and minds were wide open to the realities of spiritual life in Christ.

The illustration in chapter 2 of Jonathan and Jessica learning the authority of the Name of Jesus is a good example of a casual mentoring opportunity. They learned to conquer their fear of demons in the context of a real-life situation. Since real life happens every day, God provided an abundance of unplanned opportunities for us to interact with our kids and relate what they were experiencing to the truths of Christianity.

Focused but unstructured time together in nonacademic settings provided the best opportunities for us to impart Jesus to our kids. Driving them to and from school, lessons, and sporting events gave us times like this. We had to be prepared at a moment's notice to discuss whatever the Lord was working into their hearts at the moment. As Peter advises, we had to be

> "always ready to make a defense to
> everyone who asks you to give an
> account for the hope that is in you..."
> (1 Pet. 3:15).

It seemed clear that we could not control the times when our kids wanted to know about God and His ways. So we assumed the roles of "tutors-in-waiting" toward them by allowing their windows of receptivity to determine the times and occasions of our spiritual discussions with them. Not that we never initiated these discussions; we did, and sometimes successfully. But more often we waited in a listening mode until they raised the heart issues they wanted to share, then we responded.

> More often we waited in a listening mode until they raised the heart issues they wanted to share, then we responded.

> Lynn also developed the practice of sitting with each of our kids on their beds before they went to sleep and intentionally engaging them in casual conversation.

These spiritual discussions often happened in the car, but also casually occurred as we took walks together, or trudged through family clean-up days, or discussed what happened in church that morning. These times worked best when we interacted with just one child, isolated physically from the others. Lynn initiated this practice in our family. In this setting, the child-adult dynamics changed, resulting in an atmosphere more open to meaningful conversation. Away from other siblings, each child more readily opened inner life issues to us.

Lynn also developed the practice of sitting with each of our kids on their beds before they went to sleep and intentionally engaging them in casual conversation. In this safe, nonthreatening environment, they often felt comfortable to start sharing their hearts with her, thereby permitting her to speak with gentle spiritual wisdom into the issues they were facing. These times would frequently end with prayer, once again providing opportunity for them to witness the effectiveness of inviting the Lord to enter situations. (Of course it didn't hurt that these special moments extended their bedtimes! But we all know our own kids aren't capable of base motives like of thing.)

OF COURSE, IT'S BEEN DONE BEFORE

This notion of casual mentoring is not new, of course; we did not invent it. In Deuteronomy 6, Moses mentions specific ways in which the Word of the Lord should be transmitted from one generation to the next:

> "And these words...shall be on your
> heart; and you shall teach them
> diligently to your sons and shall talk of
> them when you sit in your house and
> when you walk by the way and when
> you lie down and when you rise up"
> (Deut. 6:6-7).

Parents must be living what they wish to transmit.

Note first that those who teach (i.e. the parents) must first be living what they're trying to impart to their offspring: "And these words...shall be on your [the parental instructor's] heart." Parents must be living what they wish to transmit. In fact we end up spiritually transmitting what we are living anyway, so let's determine to live and transmit Jesus through our deeds and words!

Moses then commands what appears to be a more informal instructional setting, similar to our casual mentoring concept.

He begins by stating his goal: "and you shall teach them [God's words of truth] diligently to your sons." Then he enumerates particular but common, familiar settings in which the instruction should take place:

- when you sit in your house;
- and when you walk by the way; and
- when you lie down, and when you rise up.

These specifics imply teaching settings separate from the distractions of other people and activities. Particularly mentioned are periods of rest and leisure in the home, walks together (would a modern application be riding in the car together?), and moments at bedtime and awakening from sleep. Might these be God-given clues to times of special receptivity in our youth — times of peak openness when they can receive spiritual instruction and impartation from parents?

We found this to be true in our family life. Perhaps it is a key to fulfilling our parental call to impart what is of Jesus in us to our offspring. We want to give what we have so they can build on our spiritual attainments and achieve far more in Him than we have done.

What Do You Think?

Parents
If you are successful in holding regular family devotions, you probably don't need to consider these questions! Write your own book! But if not...

What suggestions in this chapter are possible ways you can begin casually mentoring your children?

List other opportunities you think might be effective to casually mentor your kids.

Their Soil

5

*Key Spiritual Influences
in the Lives of ECA Founders*

*H*ome-life influences and life experiences were primary factors in producing ECA leaders. But it would be absurd for us to imply that the founders of ECA burst into ministry in their mid-teens without the influences of other spiritual sources. God formed them through the imperfect parenting they received, but He also shaped them substantially through several other means. This chapter examines these in some detail.

OUR STRANGE CHURCH

Those familiar with Newark Christian Fellowship will agree without hesitation that we are "unusual," which is a kind way of saying we are weird. We admit it. Lynn and I were college students in our early twenties when we almost unintentionally planted this church in 1972 as a praise meeting in our living room in Newark, Delaware. No great vision compelled us; our group started, frankly, as a matter of need. After failing to find an expression of church locally that resembled how church looked to us in the documents of the New Testament, we decided to try doing church on our own. (As we recognized God was actually making us our own church, we sought and received spiritual oversight from two mature congregations, a "covering" for which we were very grateful.) As we bumbled through those early years, God was merciful and gracious, and in 1978 we became a real incorporated church.

It is worthwhile to examine the nature of our church because our kids were reared in its kind of spiritual DNA and have replicated that DNA in large measure through their ministry. Raised spiritually in what began as a young adults church, they naturally reproduced that phenomenon. It has been easy for them to develop an unusual expression of Christianity attractive to youth because they were spiritually raised in one.

NCF was a church planted by young adults for young adults. Not that we barred older adults from attending; but our countercultural church style appealed much more to people under age twenty-five. For most of the seventies we did not sit in chairs but on the floor in concentric circles. We'd simply push all furniture to the sides of the room (or carry it out completely) and sprawl out comfortably. In those early years of mobile venues, we'd store huge rugs wherever we met and roll them out when we gathered. The setting was intentionally informal and generated an atmosphere much like a huge, friendly family reunion.

We became convinced that one key scriptural principle, found in 1 Cor. 14:26, should guide our congregational gatherings:

> "What is the outcome, brethren?
> When you assemble, each one has
> a psalm, has a teaching, has a
> revelation, has a tongue, has an
> interpretation. Let all things be
> done for edification."

We constructed our meetings around this scripture that clearly emphasizes a high degree of congregational input. We encouraged everyone to offer the others whatever spiritual gifts they believed the Lord wanted them to contribute.

Our meetings possessed only minimal leadership. No planned format governed our meeting agenda — other than praise the Lord, pray, then see what He did next! We really expected and permitted the Holy Spirit to plan what happened, and He did. If someone felt moved to start a song, that one would start it, then guitarists would pick it up and play along as we all sang. People prayed as led when a pause in singing occurred. In turn someone might testify, bring a brief scriptural teaching, or ask for prayer.

At some meetings we praised nonstop for hours. Sometimes as a group we laid hands on the needy among us and prayed for each other one by one into the early hours of the morning. We dressed casually, placed an offering basket on a table, and called no one by titles. We danced joyously in praise and worship. We ate together often and hung out as friends. We defined ourselves not as a "church" but as a "community." Frankly, we were then in many ways what is now being called a "youth church." Most of us were college age or younger. A dog was a charter member of our group.

Over years, as our numbers grew and family needs emerged, we found we were forced to develop more structural organization and definition of ministerial roles in our church life. Our services are now set up with chairs, we follow a general, but still flexible, agenda, and we pass offering baskets. We now start and end nearly on time! Yet even at this point, after twenty-one years as a church, we continue to value highly the creative spontaneity, community, informality, and mutuality that we fostered in the beginning. These values embedded foundationally in our church are the same ones embedded in the ministries of ECA. Their church style has been discipled by NCF's church style; though of course they have included elements consciously crafted to draw the youth of their generation. (And, quite frankly, they're a lot more anointed than we were!)

> These values embedded foundationally in our church are the same ones embedded in the ministries of ECA.

INTERACTIVE SUNDAY SCHOOL EXPERIENCES

Our church Sunday school also helped shape our kids into the young adults they have become. NCF is no expert at Sunday school or children's church. Believe me, we have no formula for what works. But over the years we have attempted to see Sunday school as fertile ground for training our kids in the realities of spiritual life that's normal for our adults.

We have conducted classes on spiritual gifts and asked youth to practice them on themselves as God led. We have brought prophetically gifted adults into various classes to pray and prophesy over our kids. We've had adults share their testimonies with our kids. For several years two women proactively recruited kids into a dance team they created in the church. We've let our kids create their own young worship teams, which never last very long but whet their appetites to create their own team later or join a youth/adult team when they're older.

Probably none of these experiments are unique to us, but they were conducted with purpose. Through them we attempted to create mechanisms that would create a sense of continuity between out kids' spiritual world and that of our church adults. We wanted our kids to make a natural transition between Sunday school and adult church experience.

WORKCAMP MISSIONS AND YWAM

In chapter 13, I discuss Youth With A Mission (YWAM) and its impact on our kids. Suffice it to say here that summers at work camp and YWAM experiences were greatly used by the Lord to plant in our youth compassion for the poor, a love for serving others, and a desire to reach the world for Christ.

RENEWAL AND THE SPIRIT'S OUTPOURING

In late November of 1994, an equal number of youth and adults from our church drove by caravan to the Toronto Airport Vineyard to experience firsthand the unusual things God was doing there. We caught something of God's presence available at that renewal center and started holding renewal meetings of our own at NCF in December. We began with a weekly Thursday evening renewal meeting, then went to two meetings and finally to three per week. Since then we've trained hundreds of Christians in our region in renewal prayer ministry and continue to hold renewal gatherings on a monthly basis.

What made our renewal meetings conducted in 1994 through 1998 somewhat unique was that fully half our trained prayer ministers were youth. The youth now leading ECA served the Lord strongly at these meetings by praying for those who attended from our church and other churches. Observing and participating in the flow of God's grace through Toronto Airport Christian Fellowship provided a model for them of how to receive God's love then give it away lovingly to others. Our kids also read classic revival literature and became immersed in accounts of the various streams of God's Spirit in the Church historically. This provided invaluable training in expanding their vision of what God has done and wanted to do again even "more!"

It became a great joy for our youth to know confidently that God would come and move through them in power. I believe this remarkable time of renewal in our church, when the Holy Spirit faithfully blessed so many through the prayers of the young, built into these future leaders of ECA an enduring confidence in God's ability to work through their ministry efforts as they approached Him expectantly in faith.

> It became a great joy for our youth to know confidently that God would come and move through them in power.

A "JUST DO IT" TEAM APPROACH TO MINISTRY

In 1995 I sensed the need for a fundamental shift in the ministry development process of our church. We had been primarily an elders-driven organization, relying on our pastors to generate and implement congregational ministries. But one negative effect of this paradigm was that nonleaders were cut out of the process of ministry origination and implementation. Some of these were complaining about this, and their complaints were legitimate in my view. So after seeking the Lord earnestly, we developed what we called our "NCF Ministry Working Groups: An Expanded Wineskin for Church-wide Ministry Development."

Based on 1 Cor. 12:4-6, 1 Cor. 12:28, and Eph. 4:12, this structure's purpose was to "provide opportunity for genuine participation and 'ownership' for all in NCF who choose to be involved in growing the church through ministry creation, development, and implementation." Each working group was organized on the basis of a church ministry. Our pastoral working group, for example, serves as a forum for pastorally gifted members of the church to meet together for prayer, spiritual brainstorming, and the creation of ministries to more effectively pastor the church.

The prophetic working group develops and implements ongoing prophetic ministries. The administrative working group develops organizational structures to oversee our conferences and facilitate implementation of other ministries in the body. Ministry projects are then approved by the eldership; finances are released; and the church ministries grow. We currently have twelve working groups, each with a coordinator and the flexibility to do what they sense the Lord is calling them to do.

This system strongly rewards individual creativity, vision, and initiative in the origination phase of ministry development. But teamwork receives high value also, in that an individual's vision is processed and practically worked out by a team within the working group. And together, all the working groups function as an integrated team of ministries serving the entire church.

> **Our youth were part of these working groups when they first began and still are today.**

Our youth were part of these working groups when they first began and still are today. Christian Dunn served as coordinator of our first evangelism working group. This ministry working group model trained our youth in a proactive "just do it" perspective toward ministry development. It also demonstrated to them the importance of a team approach to ministry and the need to value other ministry functions as highly as one's own. These values have transferred successfully into ECA's ministry development process as they plan, organize, and conduct their own meetings, conferences, CDs, and other Kingdom efforts.

PROPHETIC IMPARTATIONS

The years 1994 through 1998 constituted a *kairos* season for our church. *Kairos* is Greek for "time;" it indicates specially appointed moments, seasons, or opportunities ordained by God to accomplish unique events in the divine timetable (from *Vine's Expository Dictionary of New Testimony Words*). Our visit to Toronto in November 1994 was the second of a two-part salvo of the Spirit that impacted NCF and brought an impartation of anointed vision to our youth.

The first involved the divinely appointed visit of prophetic minister Harold Eberle. Known now as an influential prophet to the Church, Harold was just emerging from his radical period of unbridled zealotry for God when he came to us in August of 1994. The prophetic intercessors in our church saw visions of divine fire as they prayed about his visit. That certainly turned out to be accurate.

Months earlier, when Harold contacted us by phone to inform us that the Lord had told him to visit our church, we asked him what he wanted to speak about. "Spiritual things," he intoned mysteriously. Well...what could we say to that?

Through this man of God one hot Saturday afternoon, we tasted the awesome power and grandeur of the Holy Spirit's reviving presence. On Friday night Harold preached about the impending worldwide revival. He conducted a workshop on spiritual gifts Saturday morning. An anointed and energetic speaker, Harold was never hard to listen to. But on Saturday afternoon he began speaking to us in a way that completely compelled our attention. He was speaking with passion of himself and his failings in God, yet he was speaking of us as well. He was describing his encounters with Almighty God in a mountain cabin, under a basement desk, dramatizing (yet was it only drama?) his desperation for the Lord, his ferocious pursuit of and anguished cries for God to come into his life in a new way. Somehow, as he spoke of encountering God in his past, Harold was reencountering Him there and then in our presence. He was recounting his past yet somehow at the same time reexperiencing it! In turn Harold's voice rose to peaks of passionate proclamation then plummeted to a raspy, personal whisper.

As his word reached its climax — he was using as his text James 4:5: "Or do you think that the Scripture speaks to no purpose: 'He jealously desires the Spirit which He has made to dwell in us'"? — suddenly Harold paused. The Spirit's weight hung like dense smoke in the air. Silence. Continued silence. Harold walked without sound to his seat and sat down, still, waiting. Minutes passed. Though no one said a word to command it, all motion ceased. The spiritual stillness was otherworldly.

Without warning the silence broke as Darby, an eighteen-year-old, stood at her seat and cried out to God for mercy! Her voice broken, tears rushed down her face as she opened her heart to the Lord in a confession of her personal weakness and sin. Her utterly real words shot like a spear through the saturated spiritual atmosphere.

We had experienced seasons of repentance and occasions of corporate confession before at NCF. But this was different. The fervency in this young woman's spirit, the sincerity and innocence of her cry to Him, the piercing, unashamed vulnerability of her soul made her words different from other open confessions of sin among us. Some new thing of God was coming to birth.

Then a phenomenon we would define only later began to occur. The Holy Spirit, having started with one, began to move upon person after person in a visibly traceable wave around the room. An Unseen Presence was gripping brothers and sisters, extracting from their hearts outcries of conviction, prostrating many on the floor in loud agonies of repentance. As a church we affirmed and practiced the gifts of the Spirit, but at that time we knew little of the revival phenomena of the First and Second Great Awakenings. But it was precisely these phenomena, we recognized only in hindsight, that were taking place in our midst. God was invading us in classic revival power. No human was suggesting or directing a thing. Harold sat quiet in a corner. A divine invasion had occurred.

A DEPOSIT OF GLORY

Many of our youth experienced this August afternoon of outpoured glory. I believe a deposit of prophetic anointing was imparted into their lives and into our church that weekend that has functioned as a spiritual womb for their future ministries.

At his last meeting with us Sunday night, Harold called forward those between the ages of thirteen and eighteen and prophesied to them with uncanny accuracy and specificity. A divine destiny was charted for many of our youth that night. If they would choose to obey the heavenly visions unfolded prophetically, God would use them among the nations in unprecedented ways. I believe the foundations of ECA were established that weekend as our church was called to accept the task of releasing and overseeing our youth for a scope of future ministry none of us had ever imagined for them.

In the three years that followed that 1994 visitation, several prophets and apostles ministered to our church and independently confirmed the clarion call to ministry brought initially by Harold to

> A deposit of prophetic anointing was imparted into [the youth's] lives and into our church that has functioned as a spiritual womb for their future ministries.

In one weekend, I believe the foundations of ECA were established as our church was called to accept the task of releasing and overseeing our youth.

our youth. God was blowing a heavenly shofar over our young ones. It was time for them to emerge, to rise up in Him, to come forth in His sure courage and strength. It was time. It was time. It was time.

The spiritual significance of these prophetic impartations cannot be overestimated. The Lord used Harold Eberle and the Toronto Airport ministry to supply not only words of direction for our youth, but power as well—supernatural *energeia* — an impartation of the *dunamis* of His Spirit: "For the Kingdom of God does not consist in words, but in power" (1 Cor. 4:20). Home and early church experiences prepared these young vessels, but God Himself through His obedient prophetic ministers poured in fresh oil and ignited it to advance His Kingdom purposes!

What Do You Think?

Adults

Do you know places — churches, conferences, etc. — where you can bring your youth that will help give them wisdom and prophetic words about their destiny? If so, take them there!

Do you know of ministries you can bring into your church to help your youth understand who they are called to be in God? Invite them!

Does your church provide opportunities for its youth to become trained and equipped through mission organizations like YWAM? If not, consider suggesting to your leadership that they do so.

Don't Let Your Vision Die!

6

A Warning to On-Fire Young Christians

*B*eginning in 1994, God faithfully imparted vision and fresh fire to those youth in NCF destined to become ECA. But vision by itself does not produce results for God. Those who receive vision must do something with it! Resolute, wise decision-making plays a vital role in transforming God's vision for us into practical reality. Let's look at how important it is for young believers to nurture and cultivate their gifts and vision.

A Personal Fading of Vision

Bruce and I were young leaders back during the Jesus People Movement of the early seventies. Shortly after we got saved, we were married with the expectation of devoting our lives together to the Lord's service. We had excitement, zeal, and courage, like we see in today's on-fire Christian youth. We knew we had been called; we had purpose in our lives; and we had vision that was God-given. The Jesus Movement was spreading like wildfire in many U.S. cities. Former hippies and drug addicts were getting saved in droves. The Jesus meeting we held in Wilmington, Delaware, started out with about forty people but swelled to several hundred in only a few months. We saw no end to a great and growing future for us in the Lord's work.

I then became pregnant and had our first son, and suddenly Bruce and I were transported into a brand new stage of life. No one was around to tell us how to manage our new responsibilities, and, honestly, when the duties of parenthood started to mount up, our vision and zeal for God took second place. By then the height of the Jesus Movement had passed, and many who had been part of our large group faded back into the world. Our focus turned to doing those everyday things that seemed to be such a pressing priority. For me personally, although I didn't realize it at the time, I gave up my long-term vision of making an impact for God for the sake of doing the urgent things that made up my day-to-day life.

Of course I had to give my attention to those things, but I now see that the way I approached my situation was wrong. I spent my time learning to be a mom then eventually went back to college and completed my degree. I had dropped out of college earlier to get married and serve the Lord as a youth missionary, which was what I thought I would be doing for the rest of my life. Most of our generation of Jesus People lost its zeal and vision as the movement faded. But it didn't have to happen that way.

> You can do those important everyday things yet still maintain a future vision.

I am convinced we could have continued with our passion for Jesus when we were youth. I know that you can do those important everyday things yet still maintain a future vision. How do I know this? Because I do it now! In my mid-forties I'm busier than I was as a young mom in my early twenties. As an older mom now with five children I work very hard at home and as a pastor at our church. But I have learned how to maintain zeal, passion, and vision for my life. I know I could have learned this much earlier.

As a counseling pastor I see people from primarily two age groups — late adolescents and those in their forties and fifties. I have found it amazing that the younger ones often tell me the same things about their lives as I have struggled through myself. In fact, I often give the same advice to them as I have now learned to practice. The counsel is this: If Christians now in their forties had done some very practical and realistic thinking much earlier in their lives, they could have avoided the pain they experience from having no vision as they enter middle age. So to the youth I counsel I say, "don't let your vision die!"

In this chapter I want to share some down-to-earth suggestions with you who are in your late teens and early twenties on how not to end up having to talk to a counselor like me when you're older and have no vision to pursue! As you take your places as Christian adults, I pray these suggestions help you walk wisely and with knowledge:

> "My people are destroyed for lack of knowledge" (Hos. 4:6).

DEVELOPING GIFTS AND VISION TAKES TIME AND WORK

I have found that many people who believe in the supernatural gifts of the Spirit often have a misunderstanding about gifts, visions, and prophetic words. Many of you reading this book have probably received a word of guidance or encouragement about your life from the Lord in your spirit, through Scripture, or from a prophetic minister. Now we know from Scripture that God gives at least one gift to each Christian:

> "But the manifestation of the Spirit is
> given to each one to the profit of all"
> (1 Cor. 12:7).

We also know from Scripture that one's

> "gift makes room for itself"
> (Prov. 18:16).

This means that whatever gift God has given you will start operating — if you pursue that gift. Because of the creative, reproductive life of God in your gift, it will start to grow and make a way for itself in life so that it can be expressed.

But we must desire to see the growth of our gifts and vision, even after we have some idea of what they are. Paul tells us to "desire spiritual gifts" (1 Cor. 14:1). The Greek word for *desire* according to *Strong's Greek-English Dictionary*, means "to be zealous for, to burn with longing, to want eagerly or intensely." Its Greek form transliterates into English as *zeal*, a word implying great warmth or heat. *Desire* conveys a feeling of compelling emotional fervency that won't be denied until the goal in view is reached.

But many people, after getting a vision of the spiritual gifts and goals God has for their lives, simply sit around and wait for God to do something. Their attitude contains very little real desire at all. This passive approach is not good.

I believe there are two main reasons people react in this way:

1) They're waiting for their lives to become less busy. They think that once their lives slow down and they have less to do, they'll be able to give more time to developing their gifts.

2) They're waiting for their circumstances to improve. They think once their problems get straightened out or things in their lives line up, then they'll see that as a sign to start looking at what God wants them to do.

> Moses, Joseph, Deborah, Daniel, Jesus — none of them passively waited around for God to make them great in His Kingdom.

But the actual truth, I've found, is that they're simply waiting for God to make their vision happen for them! "If I just sit tight long enough," they tell themselves, "God will put it all together for me and my life vision will happen on its own!" Unfortunately this does not happen, to the extreme frustration and even anger of those who have this expecatation.

If we look at heroes and heroines in the Bible—Moses, Joseph, Deborah, Daniel, Jesus—we find that none of them passively waited around for God to make them great in His Kingdom. They all had to actively cooperate with God's ordering of their circumstances to experience the fulfillment of their vision. Moses was trained in the leadership skills of Egypt and learned shepherding skills from the Midianites before embarking on his God-given mission to deliver the Hebrews. Joseph seized every advancement opportunity given to him through a series of apparent misfortunes and became the governor of Egypt, second in authority only to Pharaoh. As a prophetess and leader, Deborah gave herself to learning wisdom and understanding the Word of the Lord. When she was called on to guide God's people in battle, she was prepared for her destiny. Jesus apprenticed under Joseph at home as a master carpenter and no doubt chose to spend long hours in the synagogue and Temple conversing with the leading religious authorities of His day. In this way He prepared Himself for His authoritative teaching ministry.

> Each of these achievers in God's Kingdom had to walk with God in practical ways to see their vision become reality.

Each of these achievers in God's Kingdom had to walk with God in practical ways to see their vision become reality. There was work and a certain amount of planning involved. Sure, God brought them to their destiny, sometimes through unforeseen and uncomfortable circumstances. But they were actively taking steps all along the way, cooperating with what God wanted of them in every situation.

Unfolding of vision takes planning, work, holding onto the vision, and paying dues to see it happen. Paul spoke this truth to young pastor Timothy:

> "For this reason I remind you to fan into flame the gift of God, which is in you through the laying on of my hands. For God did not give us a spirit of timidity, but a spirit of power, of love and self-discipline." (2 Tim. 1:6)

Paul wanted Timothy to do something active to stir up the gift of empowerment God had placed into him.

God does not give us a spirit of just waiting around being fearful to move in any direction. He gives us a spirit of power — ability — to move forward and step into those decisions and experiences that will help us arrive at the fulfillment of God's vision for our lives.

EXPLORE YOUR OPTIONS TO DISCOVER GOD'S WILL

Finding your vision and holding onto it is a process that unfolds over time, so you've got to learn to have patience with yourself. Like Abraham or Moses, you might get a fantastic original prophecy, but then you need to actively explore the details of how that prophecy should happen. This can be discouraging unless you have a correct attitude.

> Finding your vision and holding onto it is a process that unfolds over time, so you've got to learn to have patience with yourself.

We've all seen people who enjoy going to many different stores and trying on different clothes to see what they like. They may not even buy anything that day. They simply enjoy and learn from the experience of shopping.

That's the attitude we need to develop when exploring our gift and vision options. Discovering your gifts and the way they fit into your personality is like trying on several kinds of clothes. You can enjoy the process because not every article of clothing you try on has to fit perfectly. Once you change your attitude from "I must find my gift this minute" to enjoying the discovery process, the anxiety and frustration will evaporate.

This process is part of what molds our character into maturity and Christ-likeness. It helps us to discover what gifts we have and what gifts we don't have. If you persistently pray for physical healing over a long period of time but no one ever gets healed, you can reasonably conclude you haven't been given the gift of healing. But if you find that when you explain a portion of Scripture to people, they end up thanking you for helping them see the truth clearly, it's likely that God has given you a gift of teaching. An increasingly clear recognition of your gifts combined with practice will prepare you for the eventual fulfillment of your vision.

My daughter, Jessica, learned to grasp this idea of exploring to discover gifts and life destiny. Jessica studied to be a ballet dancer from age eight. Hours turned into years of discipline until she became an accomplished performer. But at age seventeen, she started developing hip problems — nothing serious for a nondancer but very worrisome to someone challenged daily by the rigorous demands of professional ballet. It looked to her like God was closing the door on her future as a ballet dancer. At that point she could have become despondent, concluding that God had let her down in the one and only thing she was trained to do. The temptation would have been for her to become depressed, lose vision, and not move in any direction.

But Jessica started looking at other options. She covered this exploration process with prayer, received counsel from trusted people, and asked the Lord to clarify or redefine the vision she felt God had first given to her. Now she is moving toward an adjusted vision that still includes dance, but also other areas of artistic endeavor. God, she believes, has made His vision for her much clearer and filled it with even greater potential to accomplish things for Him. Jessica understands and is using the process of exploration to find her gifts and destiny.

In our Christian lives, no type of training or temporary job God gives us to do is wasted.

In our Christian lives, no type of training or temporary job God gives us to do is wasted. We learn something about ourselves through each step God sets in front of us. And with each piece of self-knowledge and experience comes a more precise and closer reaching of God's vision for us. In reality, the goal of our lives is not merely reaching the vision. Indeed, the process of exploring directions in life is equally as important to our growth in Christ. It actually molds us into who we will become when we do reach that fulfillment of our life vision from God.

ACTIVELY PREPARE FOR YOUR GIFTING AND DESTINY

Let's suppose you've been called to be a missionary to China. You've had words spoken over you prophetically, and your spirit has gladly agreed. Then you wait for months, even years, but nothing happens. You find you're no closer to being a missionary to China than when you first received the call.

Your problem may be that you don't understand that it takes many small steps to get to the fulfillment of your destined vision. You can in fact do quite a lot to prepare before you reach the destiny of being a missionary to China. You can begin to learn Chinese; you can get to know Chinese foreign students at a nearby university; and you can read up on modern Chinese culture. You can take short-term mission trips, perhaps to Chinese-speaking areas. These are examples of practical steps of preparation that are in your power to take. This is important, because if you ignore these practical steps given by the Holy Spirit, you may get to China but not be prepared to carry out your mission and conclude that God has let you down.

Prov. 16:9 tells us that, "the mind of man plans his way, but the Lord directs his steps." This verse can be understood in several ways, but I believe it is saying that God expects us to plan — to do all that we're able to do to move toward a certain goal. This is encouraging; it promises us that God will reward our prayerful planning by stepping in and directing our actions. Once we make our plans and do what we can, we can expect that God will direct our steps, adjust us as He wills, and set us on the right path toward the fulfillment of His vision for us. It is often said, "if we fail to plan, we are planning to fail," and it's not God's fault if we don't get where we're supposed to go. God gets blamed for a lot of things that are due to our own irresponsibility!

I know of a couple who had tremendous passion and zeal to be missionaries. Over time they decided that God was calling them to minister in a foreign non-English speaking nation. They sold all their belongings, took their two young daughters and the cash they had on hand, and drove south. This may sound very spiritual — and by grace God may occasionally prosper an action like this — but it turned out to be disastrous for this young family. They were going into a region of the world they didn't know, to a people whose culture they hadn't learned about, and they couldn't even speak the language. They had no training for carrying out their mission and no financial support to pay for daily living costs.

> God gets blamed for a lot of things that are due to our own irresponsibility!

> Once we make our plans and do what we can, we can expect that God will direct our steps, adjust us as He wills, and set us on the right path toward the fulfillment of His vision for us.

Their trip was a tortuous time, resulting in severe negative consequences. They never adjusted to the culture, the wife suffered emotional problems, and one of their daughters almost died. They came back to the States with a crushed vision and confused minds. Did it have to happen that way? Did God let them down? Was their vision not true? I'd say that their vision was true, but they didn't understand preparation and the process of making a vision a reality. I do not believe God let them down. They let themselves down and nearly perished spiritually because of lack of knowledge. We need to prepare ourselves as completely as we can in ways that contribute to the completion of our vision.

KEEP YOUR VISION ALIVE

God's part in bringing a vision to pass is to reveal His vision to us. Our part is to nurture that vision in our hearts, pray over it, write it down, speak it out, and practically prepare for its fulfillment. We need to tend our life vision in our own hearts. The Lord instructed the prophet Habakkuk to actively nurture the vision given to him by writing it down and reading it:

"Write the vision and make it plain on tablets, that he may run who reads it" (Hab. 2:2).

> "Write the vision and make it plain on tablets, that he may run who reads it" (Hab. 2:2).

In 1 Tim. 4:14, Paul tells the young pastor: "Do not neglect your gift, which was given you through a prophetic message when the body of elders laid their hands on you." Why would Timothy need a warning not to neglect a gift God had already given to him? I believe it was because if he had neglected his gift, it would not have grown into visibility and full usefulness. It was Timothy's responsibility to keep his vision alive, to use his gift, and grow its effectiveness through the grace of God until finally his vision came to pass.

You need to do this even at this early point in your life. Don't make the mistake I made in my early twenties when I let my vision die away because I was so caught up with being a mom and taking on adult responsibilities. While not neglecting these new duties in my life, I should have continued to nurture my vision, prayed for how I could take preliminary steps toward its fulfillment, and prepared myself in as many ways as possible.

THE REST OF THE STORY

Because God stayed with me, my vision for Kingdom work was rekindled as I decided to go to graduate school to pursue a masters of counseling degree, which I received in 1987. Faced then with devoting my skills either to the secular or spiritual realm as a career choice, I accepted a position working in our church. My original zeal to serve the Lord by pastoring His people finally came into reality as I began laboring to bring the healing of Jesus to wounded adults and youth. But there was a gap of fifteen years between my salvation and the beginning of the time I started working full-time for God.

Certainly He used all that happened during that gap to train me through parenting and other experiences that matured my character. And I am grateful He did. But I know I neglected my original vision during those years. You don't have to let your vision lie dormant like I did. I pray God will show you how to keep it alive and working toward its completion in your life.

Please consider the "What Do You Think" questions on the next page.

What Do You Think?

Youth

What do you want to accomplish in your life? What things are burning in your heart to do? Write these desires down (maybe start keeping a journal of your thoughts and dreams from God) and refer to them often so that the tyranny of the urgent everyday responsibilities does not eclipse those things God has called you to do.

If you think you might have a spiritual gift, what should you begin to do? How can you tell if you have the gift you think you have?

Is there any way you can start preparing for the vision you wrote out? Think of some ways and jot them down.

Even if you can't do anything practical right now to prepare for your vision, what can you do to keep it alive?

Part

2

"Youthicizing"
Our
Churches

*T*o this point we have traced some of the formative influences that we believe shaped the spiritual raw material in those destined to lead ECA. We've attempted to highlight God's gracious influences and His delightful transformation of human weakness into divine strength. We've identified the call of God on the Joshua Generation, which is currently arising into ministry prominence. We've examined some home influences that nurtured and released our youth into places of significant ministry in our church and beyond. We've traced key spiritual influences inside and outside the home that helped form the character and ministry style of the ECA founders. And we've emphasized the importance of youth cultivating God-given gifts and visions so they don't fade with the arrival of adult responsibilities. The chapters that follow offer practical suggestions to help our churches become more youth-friendly.

For the sake of argument, let's choose to view our churches as "cultures" — groups of people connected by a common religious bond. Anthropological research tells us that cultures fall into two basic categories: continuous and discontinuous. These terms identify how successfully people groups learn to transition from their youth into adult roles. A continuous culture is one that provides a natural continuity between the youth and adult stages of life. A discontinuous culture is one that fails to offer that continuity; its youth have no easy, normative way to transition into adult roles. Therefore they often rebel against adult cultural norms to gain identity and significance elsewhere.

If we accept that churches can be viewed as cultures, it is fair to say that our purpose in the second section of this book is to identify why most American churches have acted as discontinuous cultures resulting in youth alienation. We also suggest specific ways churches can be transformed into continuous cultures, where youth can effectively transition into adulthood with a minimum of rebellion and experimentation with the world.

We certainly do not believe that our proposal is a formula that will work in every church setting. Indeed, others may have discovered much more effective ways to create continuity between youth and adult phases of church life. All we offer here is what God has demonstrated to be true for us in our church. We hope and pray these conclusions will help you as you seek to present Jesus to youth and incorporate them into your churches.

Identifying Potential On-Fire Youth

7

I am convinced there is no list of unmistakable personality traits that identify potential ministering youth. In this God seems to delight to frustrate the wisdom of the wise so His grace receives all the credit. As we observe the lives of various youth in Scripture destined to minister in significant ways, their traits as young people are not uniform. There is great diversity in personality characteristics among those God called to significant places of ministry. Yet I believe there is also a clearly defined common denominator among them.

LEADERS FROM VARIED BACKGROUNDS

If you examine the life of Daniel, you could conclude that young leaders demonstrate the marks of personal purity, courage, wisdom, and remarkable achievement. If you look at Gideon, by contrast, you might say young leaders manifest fearfulness, hesitation, doubt, and the need for repeated reassurance. Should you use Samuel as an example, you might assert that young leaders are dedicated to the Lord's service by a godly parent even before birth and start to know and serve Him as a very young child. But if you select Moses as your illustration, you might decide that young potential leaders must undergo tremendous trial and breaking for an extended period of time before being released into ministry at a mature age. Although we know nothing of the

> There is great diversity in personality characteristics among those God called to significant places of ministry.

backgrounds of female ministers like Deborah, the prophetess/leader of Israel (Judg.4:4), Phoebe, Paul's highly recommended associate in ministry (Rom.16:1-2), or Priscilla, who taught the Scriptures to the eloquent Apollos (Acts 18:26), we can be certain each of their stories would show us something unique about the way God trains His ministers.

All of these examples reveal divine truths worked out through real human lives. In Daniel and Samuel we observe the truth that God is faithful and well able to keep and bless those young ones entrusted into His care. These young men never experienced the prodigal syndrome we often see in the lives of young Christians. But in Moses and Paul we do see evidence of just this pattern of departure from, then reconciliation to the purposes of God. The principle at work here is Romans 8:28 once again — that God causes all circumstances to work together to shape the unfolding of our destinies.

Circumstances of birth and environment neither qualify nor disqualify youth from on-fire ministry in God's Kingdom.

The lives of Gideon and Timothy demonstrate that God in fact does take those the world calls weak to shame the strong by replacing their weaknesses with His divine power. And in David, God took a person of insignificance, the least and youngest of the family, and surprised everyone by selecting this nobody to be His anointed musician-warrior-shepherd-king!

So what are we to conclude? I believe we may say confidently that God can choose to gift any kind of young person — the noble and pure, the weak and sin-prone, the impulsive, the deliberate, any and all — with a leadership call to ministry. Circumstances of birth and environment neither qualify nor disqualify youth from on-fire ministry in God's Kingdom. We must train ourselves therefore to see youth not after the flesh but in Christ as we search for God's future church leaders.

ONE COMMON DENOMINATOR

This said, I believe that there is a common denominator in the lives of young God-called leaders that can be recognized by those looking for it. Each potential on-fire young leader, in my view, will evidence a spiritual trait that Jesus refers to in the fourth beatitude:

> "Blessed are those who hunger and
> thirst for righteousness, for they shall
> be filled." (Matt. 5:6)

There it is. That's the identifying spiritual mark we must look for — intense, concentrated hunger and thirst for God. In all the spiritually impassioned young people I have mentored and known, particularly those whom God has raised into leadership, I have seen this compelling curiosity and intense desire to know God, to ponder His ways, and to understand His thoughts through diligent study of Scripture. Whether raised in a doctrine- or experience-oriented Christianity, or even no Christianity, all exhibit this intense drive to make sense of God in real life.

I suspect that most children, youth, and adults are naturally hungry for God; after all, all humans are created in His image. We all have God-shaped holes in our hearts, and whether or not we realize it our hearts long to be filled with Jesus, the true Image of the Father. If a church's youth are not displaying spiritual hunger, perhaps it is because that church is serving such tasteless spiritual slop that the poor kids have lost their appetite. We must give serious thought to youthicizing (yes, it's a specially coined word you won't find in your dictionary!) our churches so we stimulate kids' innate hunger for God. We must serve them spiritual food that tastes good to their spirits and makes them hunger for more of the true Bread of Life.

I believe a good first step in nurturing and releasing on-fire youth in our churches is to locate, by God's leading, that one kid (or hopefully more) who is genuinely hungry for God. Spiritually discerning adults will be able to recognize the signs of this hunger, even in very young kids. Then by God's leading, find

> In young people, particularly those whom God has raised into leadership, I have seen compelling curiosity and intense desire to know God, to ponder His ways, and to understand His thoughts through diligent study of Scripture.

ways to feed that spiritual hunger. That's where to begin — with one or more hungry youth.

BUT WHAT IF WE DON'T HAVE EVEN ONE?

At this point you may be thinking that your youth group doesn't have even one kid who demonstrates this kind of spiritual hunger and thirst. What should you do?

> Never ease the prayer pressure until your prayer objectives are thoroughly secured!

Step one is pray! How much do you want to see your kids on-fire for God? If you want this fervently, then pray fervently. Be relentlessly persistent. Pray until you see the answer manifested, and then pray some more so the enemy doesn't succeed through counterattack in stealing away the implanted seed. Never ease the prayer pressure until your prayer objectives are thoroughly secured!

Pray with specificity; ask the Lord for prayer targets customized to those you are praying for. If, for instance, you identify apathy as a prevailing attitude among youth in your church or home, then ask in bold faith for the Lord to lift that from them. Any sinful attitude — rebellion, immorality, fear, hatred, pride, etc. — should be approached in the same way. Remember that supplicational prayer is the creative exertion of real spiritual power that generates sufficient spiritual force over time to produce the desired results. The key here is "over time." Supplication involves the exertion of patient and persistent on-going prayer pressure. When God's will is clearly known (which it is in this case), the desired result of prayer is assured, but we must still do the persistent prayer work that acts as His means to produce His desired end.

Further, I highly recommend employing an aggressive spiritual warfare approach in conjunction with supplication. Unless the Lord clearly shows you otherwise, presume there is a demonic component to the suppression of your youth's spiritual hunger. In 2 Cor. 4:4 Paul identifies a demonic cause for unbelief: "...the god of this world has blinded the minds of the unbelieving..." We must not overlook this warfare dimension in our prayer labor for our kids. And don't get too perfectionistic here. Someone has said, "When in doubt, cast it out!" While "discernment" of something demonic can be the product of an overactive spiritual imagination, I believe it is better to loose spiritual influences that simply may be there, even if they are not.

Think of it this way: if you take time to expel demonic entities that really aren't there, you've lost nothing but some energy. But if demons genuinely are at work, you've begun to uncover them and break their hold over your kids by praying from a warfare perspective. I have come to believe that the most balanced and perhaps mature form of praying involves both the breaking of the negative (expelling demonic influences) and the building of the positive (asking the Lord to come into the situation and change it). Neither should be neglected.

Another focus of prayer is asking God to provide a specific menu of spiritual foods for youth who are not yet hungry for Him. He knows exactly what platter of spiritual delicacies needs to be set before each kid to awaken spiritual hunger. I encourage you especially to guard your heart against writing off any youth. A kid's

> Employ an aggressive spiritual warfare approach in conjunction with supplication. Unless the Lord clearly shows you otherwise, presume there is a demonic component to the suppression of your youth's spiritual hunger.

> Saul, the early Church's most intense enemy, became Paul, her greatest apostle. Let your prayer be just as faith-filled for the youth who appear most hardened as for those you think are nearest the Kingdom.

hunger for the Lord may be hidden, but it still exists. Saul, the early Church's most intense enemy, became Paul, her greatest apostle. Let your prayer be just as faith-filled for the youth who appear most hardened as for those you think are nearest the Kingdom.

SPIRITUAL POISONS

Have you ever considered that it may be your family and church — not the world or the devil — that are literally causing youth to lose their spiritual appetites by feeding them poisonous spiritual foods? Please take a moment to look objectively at this. We can take authority over every demon on the planet and keep our kids cloistered and nearly imprisoned in our homes and churches, but if the problems are in our homes and churches, we're sunk. The following poisons often turn youth always from the Church and even the Lord:

- adult hypocrisy;
- belittlement of / disrespect for kids;
- adult domination / inappropriate control;
- religious traditionalism and apathy;
- behavioral inconsistency or dishonesty.

If this fare constitutes the spiritual food youth eat in our families and churches, is it any wonder they have no real spiritual hunger? They've lost their appetites because the gruel they've had is at best tasteless, at worst toxic. Repentance by parents, church leaders, and perhaps entire congregations is in order to rid these poisons from the spiritual table. Church leaders will need courage to call adults in their churches to repent from serving up these spiritually poisonous foods.

I have found that youth will normally emulate the attitudes and behaviors of genuine Christian adults. If we expect our youth to demonstrate hunger and reality in their faith, we must first demonstrate these qualities in our own lives. Repentance from spiritually toxic attitudes and behaviors will go a long way to restore spiritual hunger first in ourselves, then in our kids.

By God's grace, aggressive prayer and repentance from sinful attitudes will stimulate spiritual hunger in your youth, leading them to the Lord in salvation and radical commitment to Kingdom living.

THEN WHAT?

After locating one or more spiritually hungry kids, structure a shaping process for their spiritual development. This discipleship should personal mentoring, inclusion in meaningful ministry activities, and exposure to other fervent ministering youth in your area or region.

We've found that one of the great benefits of youth conferences held by ECA or similar youth ministries is the extended period of focused time during which youth attendees can observe, hear, and participate in worship with hundreds of other spiritually hungry youth. Youth will listen to peers who look, dress, and sound like them. And once they trust those who are speaking to them, they often open

> If we expect our youth to demonstrate hunger and reality in their faith, we must first demonstrate these qualities in our own lives. Repentance from spiritually toxic attitudes and behaviors will go a long way to restore spiritual hunger first in ourselves, then in our kids.

their spirits to the spiritual impartation and transfer of Christ's life through imitation that is so vital to all Christian growth.

Also, once spiritually hungry youth learn they have counterparts all around the nation and the world, they do not feel so isolated at home in their spiritual zeal and can be more easily nurtured and trained into ministry and leadership. Of course it helps as well to be exposed repeatedly to the fire of a dynamic youth revival conference, and to maintain relationship with other dedicated youth from other churches. I would urge parents and youth pastors to make certain this close association with spiritual peer role models happens as frequently as possible throughout the year.

> Be exposed repeatedly to the fire of a dynamic youth revival conference, and to maintain relationship with other dedicated youth from other churches.

Taking your church youth to a dynamic Christ-centered youth meeting or conference like ECA's helps mature Christian youth but also serves to spark spiritual fire in unsaved and uncommitted youth. ECA always does much pre-conference spiritual warfare and intercession targeting the unsaved and uncommitted youth who attend. Therefore a mantle of Holy Spirit breakthrough power settles over the conference, and hardened youth are softened by the continual presence of the Lord. Demonic strongholds

> Demonic strongholds are pro-gressively broken down over time, and youth are transformed in greater Christ-likeness by the end of the conference.

> **Youth will listen to peers who look, dress, and sound like them.**

are progressively broken down over time, and youths are transformed in greater Christ-likeness by the end of the conference. Past conferences have revealed the "over time" nature of this sanctifying work to be very important. Larger ECA youth conferences typically run from Friday to Sunday nights. The adults in our church who work with them have attempted to persuade ECA leaders that their conferences should close Saturday night or perhaps Sunday morning at the latest. But they steadfastly insist that the full two and one half days period of time is vital for them to do their best work in God. Something about immersion in the convicting, reviving presence of God for that long, they claim, completes the transformational work the Lord wants to do in youth who attend their conferences.

This belief certainly proved true at the first ECA conference in 1996. An unsaved group of kids into vampirism didn't give their hearts to Jesus and receive deliverance until the final hours of the last meeting on Sunday night. They were scheduled to leave the conference Sunday morning. But they objected, saying to the youth worker who had brought them, "There's something here, man, and we want to stick around to find out what it is!" It seemed to take until Sunday night for the soaking of God's presence that pervaded the conference atmosphere to take full conversion effect. We stood amazed as the stony hearts of these young occultists became soft hearts of flesh and, one by one, they gave their lives to Jesus.

> **We have also found that sending our youth on short-term summer training and outreach missions has been vital to getting them revived in God.**

SHORT-TERM MISSIONS

We have also found that sending our youth on short-term summer training and outreach missions has been vital to getting them revived in God. Several years ago, Lynn researched available summer training programs and identified two or three that we felt would be a good fit for our youth. Perhaps your church could do the same.

Every core ECA minister and many on the larger ministry team derived incredible spiritual benefit from Youth With A Mission summer training experiences, particularly at the YWAM base in Tyler, Texas. The young adults on staff there and the anointed ministers who teach at the Tyler base each summer impart scriptural knowledge, personal purity, zealous commitment, and a passion for ministry that have helped fashion ECA's character and purpose. Our church has embraced YWAM in particular because of its openness to the fullness of the spiritual gifts, its affordability, and its uncomplicated biblically based philosophy of ministry. Other excellent Christian summer programs for youth exist as well, of course.

A word of caution here: We have found that young people who benefit most from YWAM or other short-term missions experience are those with some demonstrated pre-existing hunger for God. When kids lacking that are sent in the hope of sparking hunger for Him, often the result is no change. Some return even spiritually worse. So sending kids on a summer mission (or to an ECA youth conference) is no spiritual cure-all.

Parents and youth ministers would therefore be wise to honestly assess the motivations of those youth who say they want to go on summer missions. Motivation to go solely because their friends are going is not normally a legitimate reason. However, discernment is in order here. Perhaps the Lord will use poor motivation to produce a good result. Perhaps the experience will be a time of seed planting, or perhaps He will meet the youth during the mission in saving conviction and power. So of course make certain you have the Lord's direction in your decision.

Requiring kids to raise a portion of the needed finances is one way to assess their motivation to do a mission. Our church contributes a set percentage of the project cost, but the kids themselves must actively raise money for the remainder. If they are too unmotivated to succeed in this, they probably won't benefit substantially from a summer mission experience.

DOING OUR PART

God is faithful to do His part by building spiritual potential into our youth. We're the ones who fail to pray that potential into manifestation and shape it into maturity. We must accept the challenge to war for our kids through knowledgeable, persistent prayer. We must eliminate the spiritual toxins from our home and church environments so our kids' spiritual hunger will come alive. We must provide opportunities for our youth to interact with on-fire peers at youth conferences and through summer mission experiences. And we must find ways to mentor our youth personally and place them into meaningful ministry in our churches alongside adults who value and respect them.

What Do You Think?

Adults

What steps can you take if no kids in your church youth group are truly on fire for the Lord?

Can you identify any spiritual toxins in your home? In your local church environment? How can you begin to eliminate them?

Cultivating Youth Leaders

8

A Change of Perspective

O nce young people are saved we must then intentional equip these young disciples to assume future spiritual responsibilities. Most churches have no vision for youth in significant leadership positions among their congregations. It hasn't occurred to them that youth can minister so they have developed no strategies to produce youth leaders in their midst. This chapter explores how we must change our thinking about the potential of youth as leaders. We also examine how our churches can begin to make room for them, and the ways we can pastor youth into leadership roles.

CLARIFY EXPECTATIONS

Most of you are reading this book because you desire to advance God's Kingdom. Specifically, your focus is to see youth on fire, equipped, and released in ministry for God. If you're serious about this, however, the Lord may require you to change some deeply held convictions about how youth and adults should relate. If you're serious about seeing your church welcome qualified youth into ministry, there will be a price to pay.

Because the United States has the longest adolescence in the world, it is not unusual for children to live at home without crucial responsibilities until their mid-twenties. Although parents often resent this, they accept it as a normal part of life. However, this abnormally long American adolescent stage has grave repercussions. And although we often explicitly tell them to do so, we don't really expect or permit our kids to grow up for a long, long time.

Long before adolescence begins, parents should start discussing the transition to adulthood. Our own children knew at a young age that when they were eighteen we would view them as adults and expect them to take full responsibility for their decisions. Of course we would be there to counsel them, but they would bear ultimate responsibility for what they did. When children have that type of understanding, children and parents can work together over years to train, learn, and prepare together for that goal.

But preparation for adulthood often isn't done this way in America. Adulthood is nebulous, sneaks up on both parents and youth, and is seldom recognized when it actually happens. Adulthood is one of those topics that make us uncomfortable, and we would rather not talk about it unless absolutely necessary.

However, we all do grow up, and this transition in life can actually be navigated in an exciting, productive manner. Parents can learn some practical ways to help their children grow towards adulthood, build their self-esteem, and improve

> Youth are seldom given the opportunity to lead and to take meaningful, serious responsibility for steering a meeting or a group. We don't respect them enough to grant them that responsibility. We do not expect youth to lead because we don't think they can.

their ability to make good decisions at the same time. We need to phase in adulthood by granting youth more and more genuine responsibility and decision-making freedom as they grow. And we must choose to respect them increasingly as well, eventually viewing them as our adult co-workers, friends, and peers.

WHAT IS A YOUTH LEADER?

Do you respect youth? Do you truly believe they can minister effectively? You may have a problem in this area that is currently hidden even from yourself. To illustrate, what first comes to your mind when you think of a "youth leader"? Isn't your first thought that of a youth leader is a youngish adult who is designated as the pastor and guide of young people within a church? Most Christians think this way. Certainly such adult servants of God are invaluable, but seldom do we think of youth leaders as being youth themselves who function as spiritual leaders among their peers or among adults.

Because of this perception by adults, youth are seldom given the opportunity to lead and to take meaningful, serious responsibility for steering a meeting or a group. We don't respect them enough to grant them that responsibility. We do not expect youth to lead because, if we're honest, we don't think they can. Because adults in authority don't expect that youth can lead in spiritually responsible ways, youth in churches don't expect that of themselves either. Believing that youth can

> Phase in adulthood by granting youth more responsibility and decision-making freedom as they grow.

lead and respecting them enough to let them do so are missing attitudes in most Christian adults.

While traveling to churches with ECA, I have noticed that the idea of youth leadership is usually reduced to youth being allowed to do what the adults have told them to do, rather than generating any true leadership themselves. One of my jobs as a traveling pastor with ECA is to safeguard their leadership of the meetings they conduct. Sometimes this is not easy. Even though adults have invited ECA youth to come and minister, many adults are not used to putting significant trust in youth. Therefore they have problems letting our youth leaders direct a meeting from start to finish. It is my conclusion that they believe that kind of thing just isn't done in church.

It is not unusual, therefore, for adults to try to control meetings by sandwiching ECA in between their own adult prayers, prophecies, and teachings (mind you, these are youth meetings). When I ask them to allow ECA the freedom to organize the direction of the meetings and conduct those meetings themselves, I often realize that this is genuine culture shock for them. They obviously never thought such a thing was possible.

Yet ECA youth ministers are anointed to lead their peers into strong, fruitful relationship with Christ if adults will respectfully grant them the freedom to do so. We receive many good reports of youth who accepted Christ at early ECA conferences still walking strongly with the Lord years

> Believing that youth can lead and respecting them enough to let them do so are missing attitudes in most Christian adults.

later. Qualified youth can be trusted to speak to and train up their own generation. Sooner or later some in that generation are going to become leaders. Why not let Christian youth leadership come forth before the worldly variety does?

FOSTERING LEADERSHIP IN YOUTH

Leadership doesn't just happen. Youth need to know that leadership is possible for them long before adolescence begins. Research indicates that leadership skills begin to form during the critical first six years of life. If that is true, we need to provide opportunities for our kids to explore leadership roles even during that time, much sooner than their teen years.

> Providing adolescents appropriate tools for exploration of their interests is very important to developing their giftedness and training them as leaders.

How do leadership skills develop in children? The answer is unclear. Two of our children, Jessica and Jonathan, were very shy throughout their childhood and demonstrated little if any leadership skills. Both were home schooled for many of their academic years. But when either showed any indication of trying some new interest, we made certain that the resources to test that direction were available to them. Providing adolescents appropriate tools for exploration of their interests is very important to developing their giftedness and training them as leaders.

Even though we don't know precisely how leadership skills were developed in Jonathan and Jessica, we are certain of one thing: Bruce and I were the most supportive members of their fan clubs. We valued their gifts and made it clear that we had lots of respect for them. We praised them lavishly when they did anything with excellence, and gave credit to the Lord for even the most meager of their successes. When they failed, we reminded them that while God gives all of us special areas of expertise in life, no one is called to succeed at everything. This helped them view failure positively — as a tool the Lord provides to help us evaluate what gifts He has placed in us.

> Become your children's biggest fans.

Become your children's biggest fans. Give them as much opportunity as you can to help them identify and develop their gifts. This could come in the form of lessons, mentoring, apprenticeship, or team sports. Try to structure small successes for them to achieve so they develop a can-do attitude about life, and make certain the credit goes to God for even the smallest victories.

THOSE WHO SERVE STILL LEAD

> Youth with administration and service gifts are as important on the ECA ministry team as the ones who lead worship, prophesy, and teach.

Sometimes parents feel their child needs to be a leader in the traditional sense of the word — one who is in the limelight, out front, setting direction, and calling others to follow. We adults often hold to the misguided belief that true leaders are the ones who are the most verbal and control others most successfully. But we need to expand our understanding of what makes a leader from the Lord's perspective. Youth with administration and service gifts are as important on the ECA ministry team as the ones who lead worship, prophesy, and teach. The gifts of all youth on the team need to be developed, encouraged, and — most importantly — valued. We have taken much time and effort to train the ECA ministry team in this truth. As a result, the out-front team leaders are esteemed no more by the group than are the quieter, less demonstrative ones who get the prayer and

> We need to be on the lookout for these more hidden-away youth leaders and guide them into expressing their gifts.

organizational work done behind the scenes.

I take seriously the scripture that all Christians are given by the Holy Spirit at least one spiritual gift (1 Cor. 12.7). Adolescents are no exception; their gifts can often be fairly easily identified, then cultivated.

Some kids' gifts are easy to discover because they are those natural leaders recognized by everyone. Often, however, adults look no further than these obviously gifted youth to encourage the development of young people's gifts. I have found that there are other leaders among youth whose leadership abilities are not so easily accessed. We need to be on the lookout for these more hidden-away youth leaders and guide them into expressing their gifts too.

Since it is my job to help identify the natural and spiritual gifts within youth, I often rely on the Holy Spirit to nudge me when there is even the smallest indication of a gift in operation. I know that each youth has at least one gift and probably more. So I approach each youth with that understanding. Having this attitude of openness makes it easier for me to hear the Holy Spirit prompt me with communications like, "That one has the beginning of a teaching gift," and, "That one needs to be encouraged in a prophetic gift."

One of the cues that a gift is beginning to operate is that a youth will enjoy doing something in the context of the team's ministry. We usually enjoy doing the things we have been given a gift to do. So, an easy way to find out what gifts are in specific youths is simply to ask them what they like to do.

Sometimes, however, we have no indication of what a youth's gift is. I think this is when the Holy Spirit most thoroughly enjoys giving to us adults words of knowledge about the youth in our care. Elis, one of ECA's leaders, is a case in point. As a child, Elis was a quiet, shy girl, especially around adults. Yet the Lord strongly impressed on me that she was very intelligent, with strong gifts of leadership, particularly in administration. Her character was already stable, but she had little confidence in being a leader because she had had no leadership training or experience. Elis is now twenty years old and on her way to attending college as an international business major on a merit scholarship because of her high SAT scores. She heads up the administration ministry in ECA. So be alert to the Holy Spirit giving you specific words for your youth.

RELEASE THEM AND CHEER THEM ON

My job as a pastor of youth is to equip young ministers to take my place and do what I do better than I do it! I try to be a finder and an encourager of all sorts of gifts in youth and to be a resource to develop those gifts to maturity. By the Spirit's leading, I try to identify potential ministry gifts in youth as I interact with them casually through church activities. I meet personally with them and tell them what I believe the Lord has shown me they can do in the Kingdom. Then I work with others in ECA to add them to an existing ministry team or create a new place of ministry for them, as I did with Elis. Kids will gladly do ministry and do it well if we believe they can and show them how. It is time for a new generation to have opportunity to explore and hone their own gifts. We older ones need to step a little to the side and watch our younger brothers and sisters move ahead as we cheer them on. Sometimes we must

> By the Spirit's leading, I identify potential ministry gifts in youth as I interact with them casually through church activities.

get out of the way so that others can move forward.

Is this difficult? Yes. Are there times when I have nagging thoughts that I may be putting myself on the sideline? Yes. But true leadership ministry, according to Eph. 4:11-12, is equipping others for the work of the Kingdom of God. Equipping youth to minister is extremely fulfilling when I see them out there "doing the stuff."

> The freedom and mutual acceptance both adults and youth have experienced as they worked out their differences have made difficulties seem insignificant by comparison.

PAYING THE PRICE FOR MINISTERING YOUTH

There may be a serious price to pay when a church decides to become youth-friendly and grants youth genuine ministry and leadership opportunities. Some members may complain; others may leave. This happened at NCF. Dear friends of mine left the church. Some expressed concerns that we were putting too much time into the youth. Others disliked the new, louder worship music and more upbeat, rocky rhythms. Some were jealous that youth were getting to do things that they had always wanted to do but never had. Jealousy, competition, judgmentalism, folks leaving: these, unfortunately, can be the price for bringing significant youth ministry change into a church.

As a church we encountered other difficulties in our transition to youth-friendliness. Youth and adults have had to dialogue with each other over specific issues and deal frequently with ugly heart judgments. Some adult worship team members envied the freedom and creativity the youth developed and became dissatisfied with what the adults were doing. It took careful pastoral skills to manage the pecking-order problems that developed when youth began to preach and teach in the congregational setting. Some adults were more than a little disgruntled that such young ones were given the kind of opportunities to minister that they had desired (and felt they deserved) for years. However, the freedom and mutual acceptance both adults and youth have experienced as they worked out their differences have made the difficulties seem insignificant by comparison.

Historically, when the Church has been focused inwardly toward maintaining its institutional traditionalism, youth and women have not been permitted to minister significantly, particularly in leadership. However, when the Church has experienced a season of renewal and revival and is fervent for evangelism and the increase of God's Kingdom, youth have been given respect and freedom to follow the call of God on their lives. The early twentieth-century Welsh Revival, led by youth in their late teens and early twenties, is an excellent example of this truth. The insights and intensity of the these young revivalists helped spark the major Azusa Street revival in Los Angeles, a spiritual outpouring that birthed twentieth-century Pentecostalism. Youth can not only lead other youth but by their example and passion stir the entire Church into spiritual awakening.

Our church has tried to learn from this pattern. Equality in ministry opportunity for both youth and adults in our church is not an issue anymore. We realize there is abundant work to be done in the Kingdom, and all must be released to do what God has called them to do. NCF is a few years past our initial time of change into a youth-honoring church. Seeing qualified youth as leaders among us on Sunday mornings and at other times is now normative. The people who have stayed with us, those now joining, and those who will come in the future will not question this new value. They would not be with us unless they could accept ministering youth as normal. No one would want to make this church their home if they did not accept the importance of equipping and releasing qualified youth into significant ministry positions.

We have paid a price to become youth-friendly and to release qualified youth into substantive ministry. In addition to people leaving, other church leaders question how our non-seminary-trained teenagers can be permitted to preach the word, baptize, and minister with authority in personal work with others.

But we're seeing so much good fruit from what they do. Most of our youth have little interest in pursuing worldly lusts and are healthy, socially popular, well-adapted individuals. They're now starting to marry and forming joyous, stable unions. They work in loving relationship with their adult partners in the ministries of our church. Their ministry to other youth wins many to Christ and turns apathetic Christian youth into dedicated disciples of Jesus. Fruit like this has been worth the price paid.

> We have paid a price to become youth-friendly and to release qualified youth into substantive ministry.

What Do You Think?

Adults

What traits do you think a youth would need to be a youth leader in your church youth group?

Do you think your congregation is prepared to accept the ministry of a youth who is a leader? What would help prepare your congregation?

9

Youth Need Us

The Importance of Youth & Adults Relating Together in God

One strikingly positive element in the approach ECA leaders take to their lives and ministries is that they know they can't fulfill their destinies as youth ministers apart from older adults. They honor their adult friends and eagerly welcome counsel about avoiding mistakes in life and ministry. This chapter examines the vital importance of spiritual mentoring of youth by adults.

A FAILURE IN MENTORING

In the early seventies, most adult church members were not able to welcome the Jesus People comfortably into their congregations. History tells us that many from that generation of radical young believers did not continue in the faith. A major reason for this, as I see it, is that older Christian adults were not able to overlook our different customs, dress, and ideas; therefore they could not provide the loving and wise mentoring in the Lord we needed. We needed our older brothers and sisters to guide and counsel us because they had learned things in God we did not know. We needed their instruction, their wisdom, and- most importantly- their acceptance and love.

Although Bruce and I were blessed with excellent pastoral care by two wonderful older men of God, most of the Jesus People who were saved with us didn't have this benefit. They tried to build their Christian lives and ministries alone. This observation and the bad fruit it produced have molded us for this present time. We don't want to see another generation building the Kingdom alone.

AN ANCIENT MENTORING MODEL

Four years ago, our church made a deliberate decision to embrace lost youth. We were not prepared for what we received. Many youth who then started coming to our meetings had received little if any parenting. They had done things in the world that we knew nothing about, even though we ourselves had come out of the turbulent sixties several decades earlier. The kids God was giving us to minister to had problems far beyond what we had experienced.

When I trained as a counselor, I was taught not to get personally close to those I counseled. I was told that it would drain me emotionally to the point that I would not be able to continue working with them. But because of my contact with the youth God has been bringing into our church, and the love He has given me for them, I am reconsidering what I learned.

As I studied the history of Scripture, I discovered that in the ancient world each extended family of Israel was part of a larger group called a clan. Each male within the clan had a designated older male, called a *ga'al*, who would take responsibility for him in specific ways. Ga'al, translated, means "kinsman-redeemer." Among other obligations, the Hebrew ga'al had two very specific duties toward the younger male in his care:

- to redeem his kinsman's property if he sold it (see Lev. 25:25; Ruth 4:1-6); and
- to redeem and set his kinsman free if he was captured and made a slave or if he sold himself into slavery. A male expected his kinsman to rescue him (see Lev. 25:47).

The typical American churchgoer does not experience the type of relationship that existed between a ga'al and his kinsman. American culture trains us to be quite individualistic. We do not comprehend corporateness, although I believe God is trying to correct that. I believe He desires to raise up those who will act as ga'als for all youth who come into our churches. God wants to equip spiritually committed fathers and mothers in the church who will nurture the youth He brings to Himself so they can be healed, delivered, and grow to maturity. We need to be willing to carry youth in our hearts, in prayer-and in other ways-as if they were our own kinsmen.

Paul said it like this:

> "And you know how we exhorted, and comforted, and charged every one of you, as a father does his own children, that you would walk worthy of God who calls you into His own kingdom and glory," and "we were gentle among you, like a mother caring for her little children". (1 Thess. 2:7, 11-12)

The word here for mother actually indicates a nursing mother, pointing out the connection Paul had with the young believers in that city was nurturing and intense indeed. He didn't seem to mind getting quite close to his children in the Lord.

Earlier in this book I described America as a discontinuous culture that produces increase in the likelihood of rebellion in its youth. One of the central concerns of youth leaders and parents should be what we must do to make the church culture one that is continuous. If we learn to do this, youth will have a much easier transition into adulthood. One proven way to make the transition smoother is by having each youth mentored by someone older in the Lord who has similar gifts.

We have found close mentoring partnerships between Christian youth and adults to be absolutely vital in raising our youth into Christian stability and ministry and providing a continuous church culture. Bruce and I have been blessed by adult mentors like Gary Moore, the lone adult on ECA's worship team, who has laid aside his own ministry dreams to devote many hours, days, and even years to work alongside our youth and help them realize the dreams God has for them. The youth in our church will also acknowledge Judy and Rob Palkovitz, who pastor one of our youth home groups, and Mark Lanyon, one of our youth pastors. These mentoring adults have given countless hours of their personal time to equipping our church youth to grow into their destinies.

From their childhood, our ministering youth have enjoyed excellent relationships with adults in our church. Sometimes one youth has a mentoring relationship with more than one adult, depending on the area of life needing mentoring. Our youth and adults worship, pray, and fellowship together. They also minister with one another and to one another. They are partners in ministry, and they are friends.

In a friendly and accepting environment like this — a continuous church culture — our youth naturally look to the greater maturity and wisdom of their elders, and the elders provide this without communicating superiority over or isolation from them. By the grace of God there is a mutual honoring of one another. Both youth and adults submit to the Lord and to one another. Churches that teach and practice strict hierarchy in relationships may find this arrangement impossible to understand and even have trouble seeing it as biblical. But it works wonderfully for us and has fostered successive groups of youth in our church who trust adults and adults who trust youths. Developing ga'al like mentoring relationships is vital to nurturing and releasing qualified ministering youth.

What Do You Think?

Youth

Is there an adult of your gender in your church you feel drawn to and comfortable with? Pray about it, talk to your parents, and then consider asking him or her to be your spiritual mentor.

If you have an interest in a particular area of ministry in your church life, approach the leader of that ministry and ask if someone could mentor you.

Adults

Consider helping to start a formal adults-to-youth mentoring ministry in your church. Discuss this with the appropriate church leadership.

Consider asking the Lord to give you a mentoring ministry with youth, either one-on-one or helping youth find appropriate mentors.

Challenging Kids

10

To Accept Spiritual Responsibility

*T*he ga'al mentoring adult in the life of a Christian young person provides a vital link between youth and adult cultures in the church. Anointed mentoring helps create an atmosphere in which a continuous culture in churches can transfer youth into adulthood without a significant excursion into worldliness and rebellion. But once an adult Christian mentor connects spiritually with his or her young protégé, what then? Mentoring is more than modeling and teaching. Effective mentoring must provide real, exciting (and doable) challenges for the one being mentored. Experiencing success is vital to healthy Christian growth, particularly in the development of godly self-esteem and a sense of acceptance by God. Youth must be challenged and coached into spiritual achievements. The world provides this through sports and other competitive pursuits. The church must do so as well, in a spiritual — and especially ministry — context. This chapter traces the challenge issued to the founding core of ECA and how they rose to accept that challenge and grow in Christ because of it.

_____

THE DANGER OF UNDER-CHALLENGING YOUTH

I believe that most American Christians severely under-challenge their kids in terms of spiritual responsibility and ministry. There was a good reason that Old Testament law mandated Jewish boys and girls assume adult religious duties in the community of faith at age thirteen. The Lord knew these children were developmentally prepared to accept that challenge. Further, I believe they needed that challenge to develop an appropriate sense of responsibility and significance in the religious life of Israel.

Because so many American Christian teens are barred from significant spiritual roles in our churches, is it any wonder they conclude church is closed and irrelevant to them? Human beings of all ages are compelled inwardly to seek out places of belonging and significance. If teens are not permitted to fill these needs in the

> I believe that most American Christians severely under-challenge their kids in terms of spiritual responsibility and ministry

> Barred from significant spiritual roles in our churches, is it any wonder teens conclude church is closed and irrelevant to them?

context of the Christian church, they will fill them elsewhere. We've lost too many kids from Christian families to the allure of exciting but sinful challenges offered by the world. We cannot afford to spiritually under-challenge our kids any longer. We must change the fundamental way we think about youth groups, youth ministry, and the potential of youth to minister.

In 1 Tim. 4:12, Paul cautions Timothy to allow no one in the church of Ephesus to look down on his youthfulness. Timothy's age at the writing of 1 Timothy is unknown, but he was obviously young enough to be regarded by some at Ephesus as unsuited for authoritative spiritual ministry. Immediately following this instruction, the apostle prescribes what Timothy can do to overcome this resistance to his youthfulness: "...but in speech, conduct, love, faith, and purity, show yourself an example of those who believe." In other words, Timothy was to act so Christ-like in character and ministry that his youthfulness would cease to be an issue and in fact inspire his detractors!

> **ECA successfully challenges Christian youth to achieve great things in God because they first accepted that same challenge from adults.**

We have found that when Christian youth are boldly challenged to accept the radical call of Christ on their lives to sold-out discipleship and no-compromise service to Him, they respond by rising wonderfully to say "yes" to that call! And with regard to the core members of ECA, we have found 1 Tim. 4:12 to be perfectly true. The speech, conduct, love, faith, and purity these young brothers and sisters display often challenge and elevate the lives of the adults around them to new heights of passion and commitment to the Lord. The anointing of holiness, intensity, and determination they possess rubs off on whoever receives their ministry.

CHALLENGE QUALIFIED TEENS TO MINISTER

ECA successfully challenges Christian youth to achieve great things in God because they first accepted that same challenge from the adults in their church. As NCF was reorganizing its pastoral ministries into a network of home fellowship groups in the summer of 1992, we felt that Christian Dunn and Jason Latshaw (then age 15 and 16 respectively) were spiritually prepared and qualified to lead a youth home church. But both of these young brothers were wary of going it alone and agreed to lead the group only if adult mentors provided ongoing support and oversight of their effort. (This same instinct and desire to partner with adults in ministry still characterizes their hearts.)

As we discussed their expectations and how to lay foundations for a successful group, it became abundantly clear that they did not envision a "games and pizza" home group for youth. Obviously playing and eating together are important fellowship-building activities, but socializing was not in their minds as the primary goal for this group. They wanted to establish a group modeled after adult home groups and the general spiritual agenda of NCF church meetings. They wanted to worship, study and apply the Bible, and pray for each other with commitment and fervency, using their spiritual gifts. Knowing God's raw material in their souls, we believed they could pull this off, so they believed it too.

> ECA would never have taken this first spiritual step that led to the growing ministry they have today unless caring adults had challenged them to successfully accomplish real ministry, even though they were young. They accepted this challenge because we believed they could succeed.

ECA would never have taken this first spiritual step that led to the growing ministry they have today unless caring adults had challenged them to successfully accomplish real ministry, even though they were young. They accepted this challenge because we believed they could succeed.

Young Christians desperately need adults to believe in them, trust them, and take a risk by providing them with ministry opportunities that are real and significant. I believe young believers want — even crave — that kind of challenge, and normally will rise to meet it through the grace of the Lord.

> They are youth speaking to youth, and I believe there is no more powerful communication tool to reach those they target.

GIVE THEM SPACE!

A crucial decision made at the start of this home group proved in retrospect very important to providing successful ministry opportunities for young people. We adult leaders decided that no adult would be physically present at this new home group meeting. Instead, adult oversight would be provided behind the scenes as I regularly sat down with Christian and Jason privately to mentor their ministry. This allowed these young men to take real leadership roles and be genuinely accountable to God to receive His leading for meetings. In this way they learned how to make on-the-spot leadership decisions to run the group within the safety of a general pre-established framework. In other words, while I provided general guidance, I "threw them in the water" of ministry; and they quickly learned to swim! Furthermore, a "no adults allowed" policy enabled the youth who attended to "be real" in ways unlikely to occur had an adult been leading or overseeing the group in person. This is not to say that adult-led youth groups are wrong. Not at all. But with the "raw material" in the Spirit we had in Christian and Jason, and with our confidence level high that they could do the job, it was the correct decision for us.

This pattern of youth-led and adult-mentored ministry has marked every step of growth in the ministry of ECA. It contributes in no small measure, we believe, to their remarkable ability to produce genuine and lasting revival in the youth they minister to. They are youth speaking to youth, and I believe there is no more powerful communication tool to reach those they target.

What Do You Think?

Adults

Do you provide significant spiritual challenges for the kids in your church?

If not, pray and think, and then make a list of potential age-appropriate challenges you believe some or all of the youth in your church will rise to meet.

When In Rome

11

Jason Latshaw Speaks of "Contextualizing" the Gospel

S peaking of challenges, sometimes when adults speak to youth about Christianity, they appear to be speaking a foreign language. Youth such as those in ECA are versed in the language of the youth culture. They have a much better understanding of its particular language than adults do. This is natural. In this chapter Jason Latshaw, an ECA core leader, shares how important it is to "contextualize" our presentation of the gospel to the cultural context of those we are seeking to evangelize. Adults can apply these principles to learn to share Christ with the Joshua generation.

THIS IS EVANGELISM?

"Loquitre conadre abety rwutie? Clyrioe ejsud voutney canout! Bvourt gruy callend! Loquitre! Loquitre! LOQUITRE! LOQUITRE!"

I hope you've decided to stay me with here, but if you haven't, I really wouldn't blame you. There was nothing in that first sentence which could grab your attention or even make you think that what I had to say had anything to do with you. I wouldn't be surprised if you just turned the page thinking, "Boy, I don't speak that language, whatever it is." (For those of you who are curious, that language is just an invention of my own. Even I am not fluent in it.) Notice that me getting more passionate at the end, punctuating the sentences with well-placed exclamation points, did nothing to make it more understandable to you.

Welcome to the way we often evangelize.

A DIFFERENT WORLD VIEW

What, you may ask? Don't most of us here in America witness in English? Well, yes. But how we present the gospel to others might just as well be another language in many cases. The developments of the past centuries have left Christians and non-Christians speaking a totally different language developed from totally divergent worldviews. Think about it for a moment. Since 1800, major changes in the way the world thinks have taken place. Three historical figures in particular, Charles Darwin, Karl Marx, and Sigmund Freud, have done much to shape our current society's thinking:

Darwin taught that humans are only a small evolutionary step above animals. This belief results in two unfortunate by-products: doubt in the existence of God; and the conviction that right and wrong are not absolute laws but mere evolutionary developments. Marx taught that large government systems, not the individuals within those systems, are responsible for the evils in the world. Therefore, individuals can begin to avoid and ignore personal responsibility. Freud developed ridiculed the idea of God and nearly reduced the idea of absolute morality to a type of neurosis. I am not saying that these three shapers of modern thought never had any valuable ideas. There was some truth in all of their theories. But the sum total of their work and influence helped produce a culture in which the essential concepts of Christianity have no meaning to the vast majority of those raised in the philosophy of modern culture.

Looking back at the contributions of Darwin, Marx, and Freud, is it any wonder, for instance, that the concept of sin has lost its power to influence the attitudes and behaviors of Americans? "What is this talk of 'sin?' We are all slightly more than animals anyway. Anything that we do that may be wrong is because we are raised to do such a thing by the system in which we live. And this incessant need to be perfect is really just a result of an over-zealous father who disciplined you too much while you were working out your Oedipal issues. And this isn't even beginning to broach the subject of toilet-training. So if there is no sin, why do I need a savior? What do I need to be saved from? And with no need to be 'saved,' who needs Jesus? For what? Oh sure, Jesus might have been a wise man who gave some good insight about living, just like Buddha or Confucius, but really, are you saying he is God? How do we know there even is a God? Listen, I appreciate that you find comfort in this story of Jesus dying and all that, and if it helps you deal with your psychological problems, fine, but it's just not for me."

This is a far cry from the glorious gospel that the apostles proclaimed and turned the ancient world upside down. The basic message of the gospel has been robbed of its meaning. The two languages spoken by Christians and non-Christians are as different as Chinese and English.

WHY ISN'T OUR WITNESS MORE EFFECTIVE?
Despite this problem, God has given us a promise about evangelism, and God's promises are always true and forever. Isa. 55:10-11 says:

"As the rain and the snow come down from heaven, and do not return to it without watering the earth and making it bud and flourish, so that it yields seed for the sower and bread for the eater, so is my word that goes out from my mouth: it will not return to me empty, but will accomplish what I desire and achieve the purpose for which I sent it."

This is a promise from God. It remains true forever.

Yet, we find ourselves in the position where our words of evangelism very often do seem to return void. What is going on?

I believe that this failure is because we are no longer evangelizing in the language of our audience. We are screaming in English to native Chinese, if you will. The Church seems stuck in the language and style of evangelism developed in the 1700s, when the common worldview included a God who expected His creation to live up to certain standards. Indeed, the message at that time was really meant to win retrieve backsliders and get a firm commitment from those who had ignored what they knew to be the truth all along.

Now we are faced with the task of converting a mass of people who do not even believe there is truth at all. Certainly a new approach is needed.

I'm going to take some verses out of context. I am warning you about this in advance, so you don't feel the need to get really angry with me. The New Testament writers did it with the Old Testament

> We are no longer evangelizing in the language of our audience. We are screaming in English to native Chinese, if you will.

scriptures all the time. I am aware of the context in which the following verses were written. But they apply to what I am saying here too. In 1 Corinthians 14:6-13, Paul advises the church about the proper use of the spiritual gift of tongues. He tells them that the hearer must understand the speaker:

> "Unless you speak intelligible words with your tongue, how will anyone know what you are saying? You will just be speaking into the air. For this reason anyone who speaks in a tongue should pray that he may interpret what he says."

This, to me, is the key to solving our evangelism problem. When we are evangelizing and feel like we are merely speaking into the air and that our words are returning empty, we need to pray for an interpretation. Without it we are doing no good at all. In fact, Paul goes on to say in verse 28:

> "If there is no interpreter, the speaker should keep quiet. . . and speak to himself and God."

I believe that if we do not pray for that interpretation from God, we can actually be doing some harm by more completely confusing a person by our "foreign language."

But there is hope. Our situation is not so new after all. Paul the Apostle faced this situation when he attempted to evangelize the Greeks at Athens. We can learn from how he dealt with this situation? Did he hate them, curse them, or write them off? No. In Acts 17:16-34 we find that Paul is extremely upset to see all of the idols in the city, but he chooses to respond appropriately. Although he could have, he does not organize a protest campaign and attempt to boycott all business establishments that support the use of idols. No. Instead, he studies the culture of Athens. Growing up as a monotheistic Jew, Paul no doubt couldn't relate to the worship of many gods. But he made the effort to see why these gods were attractive to the Athenians. I believe that he walked around the city, earnestly asking God to give him a key to reach the Greeks there, an "interpretation" he could speak — that one thing that would bring the Greeks from the worship of many gods to the worship of the One God. And then he found it: The Unknown God.

FREE ENOUGH TO CHANGE APPROACH

When Paul first talked to the Athenians, I believe that he proclaimed the Gospel as he had to the Jews. But the Greeks couldn't comprehend this at all. "What is this babbler trying to say?" some asked (Acts 17:18). He was speaking gibberish — like "unknown tongues" — to them. So Paul changes his approach. He compliments the people he is trying to convert. "But weren't these pagans depraved, lost in sin, and utterly blind?" you might ask. Of course, but...well, aren't we all? So Paul, in what I believe is obedience to divine wisdom, actually compliments them. Maybe we could try that too.

Then Paul makes it clear that he cares enough about Greek culture to spend some time to get to know how the Athenians think. "I walked around and looked carefully at your objects of worship," he says in verse 23. He then begins to share the Gospel using concepts that were uniquely Greek. Paul was all about results, and he knew that the Greeks wouldn't care a bit about Jewish scriptures. So he attempts to present the Gospel through elements of their own familiar culture. He reminds them of their own altar: TO THE UNKNOWN GOD. He begins to teach about this Unknown God, using very abstract terms, just as Greeks appreciated (as anyone who has read any ancient philosophy can attest). Paul then becomes more specific, quoting Greek poetry. Yes, Paul used pagan poetry as an evangelistic tool. He recited "We are his [God's] offspring," to close his argument that we ought not worship idols but instead must worship the true living God, who died for us and rose again. This message appealed to some Athenians, and they wanted him to speak to them again. A few even believed the gospel because of Paul's evangelistic wisdom (Acts 17:32-33).

FINDING THE UNKNOWN GOD OF OUR AUDIENCE

Paul successfully made inroads into a culture very different his own. We Christians today must do the same thing. How did he do it? He studied the Greek culture to see what made them tick, what they believed, and what they appreciated. We need to do the same thing. Often Christians examine the culture around them only to find more to judge, more to protest, more to criticize. We must examine our culture to find the altar of the Unknown God. It is true that that altar will be hidden among many other false gods, but we need to care enough to search for it. We need to get that interpretation. We need to be able to quote the culture's own poets, its own history. Would you listen if someone tried to convince you to convert to Hinduism by using only verses from Hindu scriptures? I understand that the Word of God has inherent power in it, but some may not even start to listen to something so unfamiliar to them. Paul used both the Bible and Greek poetry. It worked because he dared to speak the language of those he was trying to reach.

Are you speaking a gospel that can be understood, or are you speaking in tongues? If you are speaking in tongues, pray for an interpretation. God is faithful, and He will provide it. Armed with God's interpretation, and not just your own intellect, you will be much more effective in sharing the Good News.

What Do You Think?

Adults
Have you made any mistakes as a result of misunderstanding youth culture when you've tried to share Jesus with youth?

What specific steps do you think you could take to learn to speak about Jesus in a language youth understand?

What would be the equivalent of Paul's quoting Greek poetry to the Greeks in?

Youth Tribe

12

A Missions Approach to Youth Ministry

*I*n the last chapter Jason challenged us to consider whether the words we are using to convey the gospel are understandable to our hearers. If they're not, he contends, we could actually end up doing more harm than good through our evangelistic attempts. We need, he says, an "interpretation" of our thoughts into the language forms of those we want to reach. In this chapter Lynn makes a compelling case for viewing the Joshua generation as a foreign subculture within the mainstream culture, in America as well as in other Western nations. To speak to youth about Jesus through mainstream cultural language will not reach them effectively. We must sacrifice our time and preferences to learn their language to gain access and interpret Christ to them effectively.

AN UNLIKELY MISSIONARY HERO

In 1832, a sickly boy was born in Yorkshire, England. The boy's dad often discussed with his family the mysteries and possibilities of China. In 1852, the young man, age twenty and saved only six months, signed up with a missionary board and arrived in Ningpo, China.

But the young man had not been adequately trained or efficiently prepared by his missionary organization. In a new culture, with few resources and little support, this upstart youth decided for himself how to reach his chosen people with the Gospel. He studied the Chinese people closely and determined that he, though a Westernized Englishman, would be the most effective missionary to them if he looked Chinese, acted Chinese, and spoke Chinese. So he donned the silk Chinese gown, multicolored stockings, and the uncomfortable, ill-fitting Chinese shoes with characteristic curved toes. He went so far as to grow his hair into the traditional Chinese pigtail. He became quite a sight about the towns as he limped around (because of the shoes). In a letter to people back home, he noted: "I hardly recognize myself."

This was truly a very different approach to foreign evangelism. The young man's missionary contemporaries were not impressed and could not, in fact, accept his ways. He was disparaged by other missionaries, ridiculed, and abandoned. Not only did he not fit in with his fellow missionaries, but they considered him a renegade — possibly not a Christian at all, perhaps demonized. This young innovator's unusual ways did not make sense to his Victorian missionary peers.

However, abundantly good fruit was produced by his efforts. He is remembered and praised by successive generations of Christians as an innovative missions pioneer, while the ones who mocked him are unknown to us. Over time the young man revised the Ningpo New Testament, recruited many new missionaries for China, and founded his own missionary organization based on his novel ideas.

At the time of his death, his organization had almost nine hundred missionaries working throughout China in previously unreached places. People today consider him the father of the faith missionary movement. This courageous young man was Hudson Taylor.

Culture Shock

My grandparents lived on a Native American reservation in Wisconsin. I spent several summer vacations with them during my youth. My most memorable and exciting experiences were attending the reservation powwows, which occurred twice weekly in the center of their village. I would enter the high walls of the ceremonial place holding my breath unconsciously as I tried not to miss anything. Music was pulsating around me, drums beating continually. Tribal ceremonies always took place at night. The theater was dimly visible, lit only in spurts by the moon, stars, and crackling bonfires. Dancing, storytelling, and the pantomiming of warrior feats were all punctuated by the actions and reactions of a loud drum circle. Fascinated, my attention was riveted on the unique aspects of this exotic culture, so totally different from my own in upscale Greenwich, Connecticut.

When ECA held their first conference in 1996, I recognized with amazement some of the same elements I had witnessed in those Native American powwows. ECA's worship style differed remarkably from our normal worship service as I knew it in our local fellowship's worship service. It seemed, honestly, much more like a tribal ceremony than a church service!

Experiencing something Christian but so very different from what we are accustomed to can be scary for many Christians. Although he had strongly backed our youth in their vision for the conference, Bruce had serious difficulties with some of what happened there. As our church's senior pastor, Bruce felt he had a duty not only to explain to other pastors and parents what was going on, but to bear responsibility before God for ECA's unusual actions. He was quite challenged by what he saw and heard.

ECA's first conference was a big stretch for many of the adults in our church, not just Bruce. It was a far cry indeed from the typical American evangelistic meeting, patterned as most are after the Billy Graham model. As the conference unfolded, we watched, then prayed, then watched some more and prayed some more — harder! We were definitely uncomfortable with what we observed; we felt it was a little too weird-certainly by evangelical and even charismatic standards. But we also knew that ECA's generation was in trouble and our generation was not reaching them. We wondered whether this new and very strange (to our way of thinking at least) way of proclaiming Christ would produce Kingdom fruit among generations X and Y.

We received the answer as we watched in astonishment over the two-and-one-half day conference. Even the most troublesome and wayward youth — some actively into vampirism and other occultic practices — came forward to receive salvation and deliverance from Jesus Christ! Even more importantly, most of these youth are still dedicated, active Christians years later, some on church worship teams, others leading church youth groups. Seeing this kind of fruit convinced us that ECA was on to something in terms of presenting Christ to their generation. We quickly became willing to do whatever we could to help the young Christian leaders of this next generation guide their own peers into the Kingdom of God.

We are no longer embarrassed by or suspicious of the forms ECA uses to present the Gospel; we know they seek the help of the Holy Spirit for an "interpretation" to reach their own generation. I see them as Hudson Taylors of this present generation. Are we adults going to ridicule, reject, and abandon them when they need our help? Are we going to insist they evangelize our way while a whole generation of their contemporaries is lost? Of course not. Instead, let's decide to learn from Hudson Taylor's example and from the youth leaders who know by the Spirit's leading how best to interpret the Gospel to their lost peers. Let's help them do their job. But first, let's help ourselves by understanding what this present youth culture is all about.

CHILDREN OF TECHNOLOGY

> They are children of technology. Present-day youth have been drenched with information; the result is youth who have great difficulty believing anything.

We are living in what has been called a postmodern age. Since World War Two, civilization has seen tremendous progress in science and technology. My generation was certainly influenced by technology, but the youth of this current generation have been flooded by it. They are children of technology. Present-day youth have been drenched with information; the result is youth who have great difficulty believing anything. They are bombarded daily by so much information, provided by television, radio, and the Internet, that they conclude that no issue can ever really be decided. They are skeptical about established answers to life's questions . While my generation believed that science could provide answers and solve problems, youth today no longer trust in a scientific, rational approach to life. My generation wanted to know what was true and factual. For example, Bruce became a Christian in a university setting through many discussions with a Christian graduate student in biochemistry. Bruce was persuaded that the claims of Christ in the Bible were true through this student's ability to defend the faith from a rational point of view involving the concept of absolute truth..

The current generation does not believe in absolute truth, however. Therefore they are not initially interested in the truthfulness of the Gospel. Youth today want to find what works personally for them, what "feels" right to them, what "fits." We Christians may object that this an inappropriate approach to reality, but it is the approach youth take. They recognize that technology and science have not provided the security, help, and answers mankind needs.

The flood of information youth receive daily has produced a generation comfortable with diversity. They are willing to accept many different points of view without sorting them out, thinking through them, and reaching their own conclusions. Further, they do not like being labeled in any particular way because tomorrow they may think, dress, talk, and behave differently. As a result of the moral relativism they are fed, they attempt to accept all beliefs and lifestyles without condemnation. This creates a real difficulty for them initially to accept, at an intellectual level, the claim that salvation comes only through Jesus Christ.

SOME POSITIVE TRENDS

Not everything about this generation is negative, however. There are some areas in which sociologists indicate that today's youth may do far better than my generation has done. We didn't like how little time our fathers spent with us, but

> The current generation does not believe in absolute truth, however. Therefore they are not initially interested in the truthfulness of the Gospel. Youth today want to find what works personally for them, what "feels" right to them, what "fits."

> Two factors influence a child's growth more than anything else: their surrounding culture and the stability of their home. My generation certainly blew it with the stable home. Our kids have resolved to make and keep their own new families.

instead of determining to live a better way, we went on to form a society where over forty percent of parents divorce.

Two factors influence a child's growth more than anything else — their surrounding culture and the stability of their home. My generation certainly blew it with the stable home. Our kids, though, research suggests, have resolved to make and keep their own new families. Relationships are a high priority for youth and it is not unusual for them to keep the same friends throughout their childhood and adolescent years. It's too early to say for certain, but trends suggest that this generation believes in the sanctity of marriage and are intent on going the distance in life-long relationships.

Much has been written about the inability of youth to commit. But I believe the commitment capacity is there, and not only within the context of relationships. The Joshua generation has experienced more broken promises than previous generations, so they make commitments selectively. But it appears that the commitments they do make, they keep.

Generations X and Y also like to talk about God and spiritual issues. Spirituality is important to them. They are hungry for spiritual reality and willing to explore alternative spiritual systems. They are interested in God but have not been interested in Church as that institution has been presented to them.

POST-LITERATE

The post-literate nature of society today has influenced youth even more than postmodernism. Some scientists believe there has been a major shift in the way humans process information within the past four decades. We have transitioned from communicating through the written word to communicating in the language of images. Many people complain about the content of television programming and its effects on our children, yet people do not realize that the very medium of television itself has molded us in life-changing ways.

My dad was an executive with RCA. The introduction of the television into my family's life was a major event. We had a television in every room of our home except the bathroom. Yet, for us, reading was also a high priority. We were good television watchers as well as good readers. The offspring of my generation, however, tend not to be good readers. It's important to understand that the ability to read and the ability to watch television are two very different functions guided by different centers in the brain.

Reading, the ability to decipher the written word, is a left-brain function. A person who is predominantly left-brained receives information in a certain way. Watching television, however, is a right-brain activity. Television relies on images and symbolism deciphered by the right brain, where the artistic/imaginative cerebral reside. In this century, photography, television, computers, the Internet, and electronic games have all combined to produce a culture which, on the whole, does not read as a primary way of receiving information.

> Images and pictures are the language of this generation. To effectively present the Gospel to them, we must use this language. We must present Christ in ways they culturally understand.

Youth today are quite familiar and comfortable with images and pictures, however. Images and pictures are their language — just as Chinese was the language of Hudson Taylor's chosen people group. To effectively present the Gospel to this generations X and Y, we must use their language. We must present Christ in ways that are culturally understandable to them.

TRIBALISM

Some anthropologists propose that there are many elements in the culture of generations X and Y that are similar to the era before civilization produced written language as a medium of communication. Consider youth's typical life-long commitment to friends. In the absence of stable families, they are forming their own "tribes" — tribalistic subcultures in modern society.

Remember how I noted that many elements of an ECA meeting are reminiscent of the Native American ceremonies I witnessed as a child? Interestingly, Native Americans originally did not have the written word but used imagery and pictures to communicate. Music, a right-brain product, was also prevalent among Native American tribes and conveyed a common philosophy and unity that bound tribal groups together.

If you attend an ECA conference, you recognize these tribal elements very quickly. In fact, they may trouble you as they initially troubled Bruce and me. Music is obviously the main component of communication. Drum circles may start to form prior to the beginning of the meetings. One praise or worship song can continue with spontaneous creativity for half an hour or longer, flowing almost seamlessly into another song of similar length.

Even teachings are accompanied by music in the background. At the first conference, this practice gave me the most trouble of all I observed there. I found the music annoyingly distracting and didn't believe the teacher's message could be received in that setting. I was wrong.

Music, in fact, has turned out to be a critical tool to getting and holding youth's attention. Without music, even as background for teaching and preaching, youth are likely to be easily distracted and lose focus because they understand communication primarily in right-brain ways.

At an ECA conference there are other obvious elements similar to tribal ceremonies. Many of the youth who attend look quite different from the way adults expect normal Christians to look. Their bodies display numerous tattoos and piercings. Their hair is adorned with a variety of colors and ornaments. Their behavior can be jarring as well; at certain appropriate times in meetings, young people hold up swords and other symbolic props. They draw pictures representing biblical truth before, during, and after the meetings. They form spontaneous drum circles. They dance freely — but not immodestly — to the praise music (this is very difficult for those who believe Christians should not dance). The preaching is at times highly animated and dramatic. There is an absence of rigid structure, particularly with reference to time (start and end times to meetings vary considerably from what is normally scheduled).

ELEMENTS OF A DIFFERENT CULTURE

These are elements of a different kind of culture — a culture that predates the written word. We adults can judge this generation, declare them "bad," wish they were different, and in general waste a lot of time complaining about what we're not going to change in them. Or we can accept that they simply are not like us, embrace their culture, and learn to speak about the Kingdom in their language so they have a genuine opportunity to come to salvation in Jesus.

Is this shift of perspective and effort difficult? Of course, but probably no more difficult than Hudson Taylor found as he learned the customs and language of the Chinese. I personally have embraced the culture of generations X and Y. And I find now that I can enter into worship more quickly

> Paul demonstrated that understanding foreign culture is important when proclaiming the Good News there. It's easier to understand China as a different culture than to understand that our youth today form their own subcultures.

through their style of music than I can through that of my own generation! This shows that I have accustomed myself to the normative expressions of this present generation. My heart is with them.

Do we have biblical precedents for accommodating ourselves to specific cultures? Yes. Consider Paul as he asked Timothy to be circumcised when visiting Jerusalem. Consider also Paul when he talked about the gods and even quoted popular literature while evangelizing the Athenians. Paul demonstrated that acquiring an understanding of culture is important when seeking to proclaim the Good News in foreign venues.

It may be easier to understand that Hudson Taylor's China is a different culture than to understand that today's youth function that way too. We need to grasp that contemporary youth form a culture within a culture. They are waiting to be spoken to about Jesus in a language they can comprehend.

Many adults who attend an ECA conference make the decision to embrace morally neutral aspects of the next generation. After a bit of an initial struggle, they accept the form of outreach as an attempt to reach a culture that is almost completely alien to the culture of their own generation. However, some concerned parents or youth leaders who attend the same conference look at the meeting's form rather than its content and seriously misunderstand what is actually taking place. I can sympathize with those who have concerns like this because I had to deal with my own areas of challenge at my first ECA conference. So I am not unsympathetic. But adults who come to ECA conferences, in my opinion, need to approach that setting as a missionary outreach effort. (In fact, we are implementing a pre-ECA conference adult seminar to prepare first-time adult visitors for what they will encounter.) Some adults recognize youth as a different culture and are willing to embrace the conference on that basis. Others are confused but willing to go along with things they don't yet understand. And a small minority fearfully regard some conference elements as demonic. Unfortunately this last group will not be able to minister the Gospel to or make disciples of many of today's youth.

Let me share some amazing insight I gained from a wise youth leader who recently attended an ECA conference. This youth minister and his group are African-American. They were obviously having a difficult time getting into the worship the first night of the conference. I then noticed that at the Saturday morning meeting, they were more focused and started to get involved. By the third meeting, it was clear to me that all the youth had obviously had a breakthrough in God and were thoroughly enjoying His presence through praise and worship in sync with the rest of the believers there.

Astounded and curious about this progressive transformation, I approached the group's leader and asked him what had happened to produce such a remarkable change in his kids. He said,

> Will we, the older generation, think it is more important to preserve our old personally preferred ways, or will we be willing to lay aside our dear customs in order to bring Jesus to youth?

"We just had a hard time relating to how your kids worshipped. So that first night, my kids and I talked about how we could worship here when we couldn't relate to what you did. I told them that we didn't have to connect with the music but we could connect with the hearts of the people here and worship Jesus together with our hearts. My kids decided to know the hearts of your kids so that we could be in unity. So that's what you saw. Once they understood the hearts of the believers here, they had no problem worshipping with you all!"

I think this was an incredible answer. These kids had learned to put their preferred culture on the shelf and welcome another culture into their hearts while at this unfamiliar kind of youth conference.

I believe we should learn much from this wise youth leader. Will we, the older generation, think it is more important to preserve our old personally preferred ways, or will we be willing to lay aside our dear customs in order to bring Jesus to youth? I believe God is challenging our hearts in this.

On a very practical level, our churches need to change if this generation is going to be reached and take part with us in our church services. Many of these changes are discussed in detail in the next chapter of this book, but we can summarize them here:

- We need to change our music to accommodate youth culture; we need to explore and use alternative forms of musical worship.
- We need to change our Christian jargon and learn to use language forms youth can comprehend.
- We need to communicate more in terms of oral tradition — presenting the gospel through art and drama rather than only through the written word.
- We need to change the structure of our seating arrangements.
- We need to use technology — especially computers, and the web — to communicate effectively with youth.

Evangelism to the youth tribe among us will continue as God sends missionaries with a vision to accept them and a willingness to identify with them as a subculture. Perhaps this posture will result in rejection by the larger Body of Christ, as it did for Hudson Taylor. Such is the price for proclaiming Christ. May God bless the sacrificial efforts of these radical missionary pioneers!

What Do You Think?

Adults

What elements of the "youth tribe" culture described in this chapter do you see in your church's youth?

Would you anticipate that if youth in your church were permitted to conduct church on their own according to their own stylistic preferences, adults in your church would be frightened and judgmental?

If so, can you think of any ways you or your church leadership could prepare the congregation and perhaps minimize the shock?

Rethink the Wineskin

13

Preparing Your Church for a Youth Invasion

*A*t the end of the last chapter, Lynn calls for churches to seriously consider making substantive changes in the ways they do church — changes designed to more productively relate Christ to the youth culture. If we want our churches to function as continuous cultures, they must offer bridging mechanisms to enable our youth to take their places within them in meaningful ways. This chapter suggests specific transformations in church leadership and church structure that will implement this bridging process.

A RADICALLY DIFFERENT CHURCH

Years ago the Lord spoke to Mike Bickle, pastor of Metro Christian Fellowship in Kansas City, Missouri, that He would change the understanding and expression of Christianity as we know it in a single generation. When I first heard this, I wondered how such a massive change would come — dramatically through some kind of spiritual cataclysm or in progressive phases? No doubt, because His ways are not ours, much of what He will do to cause this revolution will surprise us and challenge our fundamental preconceptions about Church.

However the Lord accomplishes this sweeping change, I am certain the result will enable His people to embrace more and more effectively the "youth tribes" on the planet. The net He is building must be large and varied enough to hold the vast diversity of humanity destined to receive Jesus in the last great gospel harvest. That vast diversity includes millions of youth. In light of His intention, therefore, we must give serious attention to restructuring our churches to prepare for the coming invasion of youth.

A dramatic and pervasive cultural shift took place as boomers started coming of age in the late sixties. Viewed as the dawning of a hope-filled New Age by its proponents and as cultural destruction by its critics, the societal revolution of that time swept away manmade institutional traditions and norms, many from the Church included. But thirty years later, the contemporary Church is in many ways still resistant to morally neutral changes in fashion, worship, and preaching styles that, I believe, had their beginning in the turbulent sixties. I believe that much of the single-generation change spoken by the Lord to Bickle has to do with the

> I believe today's Church must become consciously and intentionally youth-friendly.

Church as an institution finding ways to accommodate-without compromise of basic biblical truth-the stylistic preferences of the youth culture. I believe today's Church must become consciously and intentionally youth-friendly. Only in that way will we win them to Christ and hold them in the Church in the kind of massive numbers I believe the Lord desires.

How can this occur? How can a local church rethink its mission, restructure its ministries, and reinvent the practical ways it conducts church to be relevant to youth? This chapter suggests a number of specific ways to accomplish these objectives.

A MANDATORY PARADIGM SHIFT

> Youth will never freely express their gifts in the Lord if they feel the spiritual climate of their church is not youth-friendly

Before any lasting change can occur, local church leaders must experience a fundamental shift in their presuppositions about youth and church ministry. The very title of this book, *Youth Can Minister*, must become an emphatic belief in the hearts of the persons now responsible for church leadership. Those currently holding church authority — especially senior pastors — must dare to become convinced that youth can share in the exercise of authority and spiritual gifts, that they can minister effectively not only to their peers but even to adult congregational members. And for that to happen, opportunity for youth to express their ministries in the absence of non-biblical restrictions must be given. Youth will never freely express their gifts in the Lord if they feel the spiritual climate of their church is not youth-friendly.

If this cognitive transformation among current senior church leaders does not occur, all the practical changes in church structure suggested in this chapter are worthless. Practical changes will not release youth into ministry without an atmosphere of acceptance. A supportive context of vision and faith from adults is needed for the Lord's grace to flow to and through the youth in our churches.

This is of utmost importance because our youth will surely find contexts of expression for their talents and gifts. They will express them either in the Kingdom or in the world. And if the world offers them opportunities, but the Church does not, guess which environment they will choose?

My oldest son is a gifted guitarist and songwriter. As he grew through his teen years and sought a venue for his talent, our church had no vision for youth on the worship team (or on other ministry teams either). Joshua therefore found the secular realm to be the only context open to his guitar abilities. He now walks with the Lord and witnesses at a personal level through his band. While I am grateful Christians enter secular arenas like this as lights in dark places, I wonder how much more impact for the Kingdom his musical gifts could have had if our church had thought differently about youth participation on adult ministry teams.

I want my kids and those in my church to be able to express their gifts with creativity and excellence in a Kingdom context. Only when the minds of adult church leaders are fully convinced that qualified youth can minister with anointing and integrity will structural changes in our churches produce truly youth-friendly spiritual environments.

WE MUST TRUST GOD'S MINISTRY ANOINTING IN YOUTH

A personally embarrassing story may perhaps help some of you parents and church leaders as your youth begin ministering in your churches. On the first night of the first ECA youth revival conference in 1996, I attended as an intercessor and an observer. Because of my trust in them and my belief that God could gift them with ability to conduct the conference with anointing and effectiveness, I intentionally had not gotten much involved in planning conference sessions. So, frankly, I was shocked by the unfolding of that first session of the weekend. To make matters worse, I knew various local pastors and youth leaders would attend this session, and I felt that the reputation of our church (not to mention my own rep as well!) was on the line.

> **As that first conference session unfolded, critical thoughts swarmed my mind concerning just about everything our youth were doing!**

As that first conference session unfolded, critical thoughts swarmed my mind concerning just about everything our youth were doing! They started at least half an hour late. They adjusted the conference room lights down much too low for my taste. Their music was, to me, far too loud and their songs repeated about a hundred times too often! I personally give thirty-to forty-minute talks when I teach, so I grew increasingly restless and angry as the session teaching, delivered by an 18-year-old with much zeal but little experience in teaching the word, showed no sign of ending as he ran well over an hour. When the teaching digressed into odd personal stories and weird attempts at humor, I thought, "surely these kids will lose total interest in his message and the entire session will end with them bored to tears and desperate to leave! They'll probably badger their youth group leaders to take them home the next morning."

But to my immense surprise, the crowd of over six hundred young people listened attentively throughout Christian's long message, then responded en masse to his fervent call-forward for repentance from sin! By that time I was on the floor between rows of chairs, loosing demons of judgmentalism from my soul while at the same time begging God's mercy for allowing this slipshod, disorganized conference to take place without my direct, authoritative involvement! There goes church credibility!

GOD'S WAYS NOT MINE

When conference youth began streaming forward to the area in front of the stage, dropping to their knees in repentance and crying out to the Lord for forgiveness and cleansing, I was suddenly and starkly confronted with my own raw pride and spiritual dunderheadedness!

Look what God was doing!

The evening session had not gone at all as I would have conducted it. I had cleverly identified scores of procedural mistakes and program flaws that I was certain would destroy God's ability to show up in power.

But look what He was doing!

He was showing up with real transforming power, doing a whole lot more with young people than I had ever been able to accomplish. A small-scale youth revival was happening before my eyes.

Did I quickly do some serious repenting!

TRUSTING GOD THROUGH THEM

What I discovered that night was that the Holy Spirit, through ECA youth leaders, knew what He was doing. I learned that I was being called to trust Him in them. What I viewed as ministerial errors the Spirit was using as weapons of righteousness.

The youth worship team's seemingly endless repetition of verses or phrases of a song in worship was actually breaking through encrusted youth resistance to the traditionalism of hymns and habitually played contemporary choruses. Dim lights enabled the youth there to feel

> What I viewed as ministerial errors the Spirit was using as weapons of righteousness

less self-conscious and more able to abandon themselves in praising Jesus. The high-decibel sound level freed them to enter more easily into God's presence by compelling their focus to be on the Lord and minimizing distractions. And the lengthy word was not a problem to them but somehow became an honest personal bond of relationship between that young preacher and other youth in the room. One of their own was speaking directly to them and revealing his heart; he was not playing a role but was sharing things they could relate to in ways they themselves shared in their own experience. Clearly the Holy Spirit flowed over that bond of spiritual connection, reviving the hearts of those young ones and drawing the unsaved to the Savior in awesome reality of genuine transformation.

I am now so ashamed of my attitude that evening. I was absolutely wrong not to trust that the same Lord Who had led the ECA core leaders to that point would be faithful to lead them through every session, every workshop, every ministry time, every prayer and proclamation, even through every unusual dramatic prophetic act. Hundreds of young lives were permanently changed for Christ that weekend; the scores of written testimonies we received confirm this. Had I self-importantly stepped in to take charge, those changes almost certainly would not have taken place. What a horrible mistake it would have been had I succeeded in imposing my vision of the conference on

> It is crucial that Christian adults not fear to allow on-fire youth in their churches to express relationship with God in their own ways. Instead of seeking to control and dictate, we must learn to support and encourage.

them. It was their conference, they were anointed to conduct it, and I was not.

If we desire to see qualified youth released into ministry that reaches their peers, we adult church leaders must learn to trust the Lord in them! They will not minister as we do to reach our peers. The Spirit will fashion through them new wineskins of worship, preaching, and outreach to enable them to fulfill their own ministry call to their own generation. It is crucial that Christian adults not fear to allow on-fire youth in their churches to express relationship with God in their own ways. Instead of seeking to control and dictate, we must learn to support and encourage. We must manifest the heart of Jesus, who came not to be served but to serve. Our youth must know we are trusting them, interceding for them, and standing behind them as they take risks for Jesus by daring to appear weak and foolish to their unsaved peers in order to proclaim Christ. We too must take a risk and choose to trust our youth.

LEADERSHIP STRONGLY SUPPORTING THEM

Without strong church leadership support, ministering youth will not succeed in your church. God honors delegated authority. What that authority permits, God will bless; what they forbid will be forbidden by God as well (Matt. 18:18). The members of your church need to know without doubt and probably repeatedly that their leadership is excited about and entirely supportive of releasing qualified youth

I oversaw our youth as they established their first youth home church. We made it clear to our congregation that this first youth home church was a valid and important member of our home church network.

into ministry.

I oversaw our youth as they established their first youth home church, and I advised them as they took that group through various stages of growth. We made it clear to our congregation that this first youth home church was a valid and important member of our home church network. When they decided to birth their own worship team, we stood behind them. When they asked one of our adult worship leaders, Gary Moore, to anchor their worship team but remain in the background musically, he graciously consented, and our leadership gave wholehearted support to this arrangement. When our youth took the giant ministry step of wanting to conduct their own youth conference, we swallowed hard, prayed a lot, then, believing their vision was from God, gave it our enthusiastic support. When we saw the need to provide some measure of consistent financial support to ECA's two catalytic leaders, Christian and Jonathan, we communicated this decision to the congregation, uncertain what their reaction would be. It turned out not to be a problem. By that time our congregation knew and participated in ECA's ministry and strongly endorsed this financial initiative.

Our youth would not have flourished as they have without partnering with our church first spiritually, then in many practical ways. It is church leadership's job, in my view, to foster that partnership through extensive communication of their own support for ministering youth. Once church members see their leaders' support, they will provide theirs as well.

Respect Ministering Youth

The worship phase of the meeting had ended. The Spirit of the Lord had fallen and many youth were quiet before the Lord, loving Him and filled with His sweet presence. As the ECA preacher of the evening started to speak, it was obvious that the Holy Spirit had gripped him as well as he began to share from the depth of his heart. All there became focused and intent as the anointing of the young man's words began to flow into listening hearts.

That night another youth pastor had brought his two-year-old with him to the meeting. As the teaching started, this toddler meandered up on stage and began crisscrossing in front the young ECA preacher, providing a distracting sideshow. Annoyed but not quite knowing how to handle this situation, the young leader continued his word. He endured this rudeness until, well into the word, the senior pastor's wife noticed the problem and retrieved the child.

Now if that ECA preacher had been an adult traveling minister brought in by the church to conduct a special meeting, do you think the youth pastor's young son would have been allowed to toddle across the stage as the minister brought his word? Of course not. Was it not the youthfulness of the ECA speaker that permitted this disrespect?

Frequently, when the ECA ministry team gathers to pray before beginning a meeting, they invite adults from their host church to join them as a matter of courtesy. More often than not, the invited adults end up dominating this prayer time; after prayer ends, ECA has to meet again and pray by themselves. Would this domination of the flow of prayer occur if ECA were not young ministers, if the traveling ministry team consisted of all adults? I do not think so.

Christian adults — leaders especially — must learn to respect the anointing of God on ministering youth. If God has raised up qualified youth in your church, respect that work of the Lord in those youth even as you would in other adults. I believe the kind of disrespect shown toward ECA in these two instances is a violation of 1 Tim. 4:12, which indicates that the church must not look down on a young minister simply because of his youthfulness.

> Christian adults & leaders must learn to respect the anointing of God on ministering youth.

> **At our church, we adults have intentionally assumed the role of servants toward the ministering youth among us.**

In the same way that we in the Church rightly honor and serve those adults who minister to us (Rom.13:7), we must honor and serve those anointed youth who minister among us. At our church, we adults have intentionally assumed the role of servants toward the ministering youth among us. At their conferences we help them administrate (the area of ministry where they need the most service from adults) and implement their specific conference vision in practical ways. We exercise a helps gift on their behalf. We run sound for them, organize their registration procedures, and provide security. Although we remain their mentors and elders, we see ourselves as called to assist them as they carry out the ministry assignments the Lord has given them. God called them to do their ministry, not us, but we are certainly available to consult with and provide guidance if difficulties begin to occur. There is a healthy and mutual sense of working partnership among our youth and adults which stems from the honor and respect we all grant one another. We realize this turns notions of normal church hierarchy upside down, but our serving our youth has released much blessing into their outreach work. It has been worth the results.

STAND IN THE GAP FOR YOUR YOUTH

During their first conference and particularly through their first year of traveling ministry, the NCF adults carried the intercessory load for ECA. Our church

> **Our church intercessory teams made the prospering of our youth's ministry a major prayer priority.**

intercessory teams made the prospering of our youth's ministry a major prayer priority. Now, three years later, ECA generates their own intercessory covering and is disciplined and faithful to do all the prayer work needed to successfully discharge their ministries. They meet one evening per week for general intercession and more frequently as conferences or major ministry trips approach. They also provide their own youth intercessory team that actively stays on duty during all their ministry events. But until this system developed, our adult intercessors carried the prayer load for them. At present we remain back-up intercessory partners.

On occasions when criticism or other forms of fleshly or demonic interference (e.g. odd misunderstandings, hurt feelings, equipment breakdowns, sudden sicknesses, etc.) came their way, key adults would step in and handle things so they wouldn't be forced to dilute their ministry focus. As ECA has matured, they've learned how to handle irritants like these themselves. Adults intercede for them now in these areas far less often.

INVITE YOUTH TO JOIN ADULT MINISTRIES

It cannot be overemphasized how rejected by adults most youth in our culture feel all the time. Particularly in churches, only adults have traditionally occupied key places of ministry. Most Christian youth, raised to be sensitive to appropriate lines of authority, would never consider inviting themselves to participate on adult

> Most Christian youth would never invite themselves to participate on adult ministry teams. Youth cannot take the lead here. It is crucial, therefore, that adults proactively recruit qualified youth to join with them in our church ministries.

> When unbelievers witness young & old, Jew & Gentile, slave & free, black & white, male & female laboring together as one in the cause of Christ, the world will give new attention to the claims of the Gospel. In Christ, the older & the younger ought to be one.

ministry teams. Youth cannot take the lead here. It is crucial, therefore, that adults proactively recruit qualified youth to join with them in our church ministries.

This is important to do for several reasons. First, it will be an effective first step in breaking down the dividing wall between Christian youth and adults. This of course is valuable in itself. Unbelievers need to witness young and old, Jew and Gentile, slave and free, black and white, male and female laboring together as one in the cause of Christ. When our loving unity becomes visible, the world will give new attention to the claims of the Gospel. In Christ, the older and the younger ought to be one.

Second, in a group with legitimate authority like the Church, those with power must voluntarily extend participation in that power to those who lack it. Otherwise, the powerless will remain cut out of the process of growing into places of usefulness and authority.

Third, inviting youth to join adult ministry teams gives them opportunity to be lovingly mentored in their gifts. Being mentored is essential to Christian growth. What better way to provide a natural mentoring context for youth than through regular association with similarly gifted adults on ministry teams?

Finally, adding youth to the mix contributes a diverse richness to the adult team itself. Wisdom and exuberance, caution and zeal balance one another. The raw passion and fire of the young can rekindle the zeal of adults, and the experience and practical know-how of adults are valued by discerning youth. Church ministries will be enriched as adults and youth combine their emphases in ministry.

Before ECA had its own worship team and produced original worship music, core members of that team apprenticed with the NCF adult worship team. Part of our strategy to become a youth-friendly church involved adding qualified youth to our Sunday morning worship team. We looked for youth who were obviously genuine worshippers first, then checked to see if they were musically talented as well. We started with two youth and have added several more. Currently the youth on our adult team freely suggest prospective songs for the team to learn and make valuable contributions during practices. A fruitful spiritual synergy has developed to such a degree that now the adults feel loss if youth don't play a major role on the "adult" worship team.

Over the past two years we have included youth on our adult ministry teams in the following areas: prophetic, administrative, altar prayer, healing, evangelism, and public ministry on Sundays at our congregational open mic. We have also listed our qualified youth preachers and teachers on our Sunday morning rotation of NCF members who teach the church. The ECA worship team leads Sunday morning worship once per month. Thankfully, we have received an overwhelmingly positive response to our youth's ministry participation.

Looks like Jonathan may be starting to take my job a little earlier than I thought he would!

We have found a fascinating dynamic taking place as we purposed to make our church youth-friendly. Soon after we invite our youth to work with us in some area of ministry, they begin to develop that same ministry among their youth church on Sunday night. For example, not long after we invited them into our adult worship team, they formed their own worship team (while not abandoning participation with us adults, of course). After learning to minister in

> It seems that our authorizing them to join us encourages & empowers our ministering youth to do the same thing among their own Sunday night youth church

renewal prayer with us, they began doing so when they met by themselves. It seems that our authorizing them to join us encourages and empowers our ministering youth to do the same thing among their own Sunday night youth church.

MAKE ROOM FOR THEIR
UNIQUE EXPRESSION OF CHURCH

It turned out to be a great thing for our youth to join with us on our adult ministry teams. They appreciated it and so did we; all in the congregation received much benefit. But their real emergence into powerful ministry came as our youth developed their Sunday evening home group into a full-fledged youth church, which now meets in our church training facility. By youth church, I mean a meeting of youth (a few adults can attend as observers but never as leaders) organized, led, and developed by youth. ECA's Sunday Night Youth Church now consists of more than a hundred young people half from our church and half visitors who come to observe the meeting. Occasionally whole youth groups from churches come to the meeting to partake in a working model of a youth-led youth church.

Out of this cohesive and growing youth church ECA's ministry team selects and equips new members. Every Sunday night they practice the worship, teaching, and ministry gifts God uses to impact thousands through their outside meetings and conferences. Along with NCF as their mother church, this youth church is truly home base to the ECA ministers. It serves as a training ground for hands-on equipping in ministry week after week.

Under leadership care and blessing, a stable core of qualified, trustworthy youth in your church could form their own youth church as well. Adult leaders could mentor the young leaders and oversee their work behind the scenes. Your youth could develop worship, teaching, and ministry styles unique to them. If adult leaders in your church would risk trusting them and turning them loose in God, I believe you would be amazed at their fruitfulness. Your youth would enjoy their meeting and tell other youth, who would tell others, and so on. They would get into God's presence in ways the Holy Spirit would show them. Many would be renewed and healed, others saved, and a growing youth revival might very well result! But you've got to let them do it their way, within the plain guidelines of Scripture of course.

> Under leadership care and blessing, a stable core of qualified, youth in your church could form their own youth church.

PRACTICAL SUGGESTIONS

There are many practical differences between youth and adult church. If your youth set up their own church, they will probably come up with suggestions on their own of how to do that. Even adults may want to examine implementing some of the ideas listed below into regular Sunday worship settings as we consider how to make our adult services more youth-friendly.

Lose the Pews!

Obviously whether a group worships in pews, in a circle of chairs, or sprawled out on the floor is a morally neutral issue. But to youth the kind of space available for their worship is very meaningful. As time-honored and beautiful as pews may be for adults, to youth they signify traditionalism, regimentation, and restriction of their personal liberty in the Lord. To contemporary Christian youth, worship is a highly physical, all-engaging exercise, in which they literally need room to move. This of course is not news to African-American and Hispanic Christians, whose responsive, physically expressive style of worship is in many ways a forerunner of what is emerging as a desirable form of worship among Caucasian Christian youth.

Youth like to jump and dance, and should be permitted to do so (in non-sensual ways of course) when they praise God. In a sanctuary filled with pews, they'll get quickly into the aisles or even up near the altar in traditionally designed sanctuaries. They'll get close to the worship team so as to synergize spiritually — add their voices and spirits to the praise and worship experience generated by the worship team.

> Place youth into a "rave" setting but fill it with praise & worship, sanctifying the setting & releasing them to experience church in a culturally relevant way.

Christian youth will follow the leadership direction and modeling of their anointed peers in praise and worship. We have seen it repeatedly. When ECA first ministers in praise and worship, youth not familiar with their passion, abandonment, and creativity are a bit stunned by their wholehearted expressiveness. Most of these novices remain in their chairs (pews) and perhaps mildly clap their hands. Some may awkwardly stand up at their seats. Initially they are so unfamiliar with abandoned worship that mostly they simply observe. Yet as ministry continues, and as the call to greater passion in worship is made, the example of the ECA worship team somehow rubs off spiritually on nearly everyone in attendance, young and older as well.

Youth participants begin to understand that they are permitted and, in fact, encouraged to express themselves freely and physically as they praise the Lord. They may jump, pump their arms in the air, and dance with exuberant joy in the Lord.

Praise and worship songs seem unending, with one discernable piece flowing into the next without much, if any, interruption. The music is punctuated by impassioned exhortations or proclamations about the Lord and His intentions for those gathered. Sometimes ECA leaders sense the Holy Spirit moving in a particular way and issue a call-forward for personal ministry. Throughout it all, the music is softly or loudly providing a uniform background for all that takes place. While this is an accurate description of ECA-style worship, it should not be viewed as a prescription for all youth churches. Each will find its own unique expression of worship.

Is this a Christianized "rave scene"? Certainly there are parallels. Youth today have grown up in the cultural milieu of rave. I believe there is nothing inherently sinful about a rave-scene environment. What constitutes any environment as sinful are the kinds of spiritual energies and deeds that take place in it. So to place youth into a rave setting but to fill it with anointed praise and worship of the Lord sanctifies the setting and releases youth to experience church in a way that is culturally relevant to them. Creating a contemporary setting encourages them to open their spirits to the Lord. Once they do that, Jesus takes care of the rest.

Lower the Lights!
Youth are notoriously self-conscious. It goes without saying that adolescence is a time of intense self-focus on physical appearance. When lights in a room are bright, zits, skinniness, extra pounds, and other bodily attributes disturbing to youth are much more noticeable. It's tough for

> Dimming the room lights make zits, extra pounds, and skinniness less noticeable, freeing youth from their inhibitions and enabling them to enter into praise and worship more fully.

youth to come with joy into the presence of the Lord when they're so acutely aware of being embarrassed in the presence of one another.

Therefore we've found that dimming the lights of a meeting room greatly increases the likelihood that youth will allow themselves to enter fully into praise and worship abandonment in front of their peers. Of course we would never advocate or permit the low lighting of a room to become a cloak for sinful behavior. Should this start to happen, the room should immediately be brightened and the problems addressed directly. We have not found that to be a problem, however. For the vast majority of Christian youth, dim lighting merely helps release them from the pain of self-consciousness and enables them to approach the Lord with greater ease.

Crank It Up!

Most youth today are audiophiles. They love (and demand) good quality sound equipment for the music that is so much a part of their lives. So if the audio system used to amplify their praise and worship music is under-powered or of poor quality, they simply will not enter into worship easily. Poor sound equipment will hinder their approach into God's presence.

Perhaps this should not be the case. But for youth we've found that it simply is, and the church that desires to make itself youth-friendly must recognize and accommodate itself to this reality. So make the investment in a good quality sound system. And once you've obtained the system, crank it up! The preferred decibel level of praise and worship music for youth is considerably more earsplitting than it is for most adults. As one conference brochure noted, describing the youth portion of this family conference: "If it's too loud, you're too old!" If we want our youth to be passionate and excited about Jesus, we'll have to let them experience a worship volume level that would quickly drive most folks over forty out of the room, if not out of their minds!

Footloose and Fashion-Free!

When Lynn and I were first saved, we felt completely comfortable traipsing into the mammoth sanctuary of our Baptist church home in sandals, tie-dyed tee shirts, and "holey" blue jeans. Although we felt completely comfortable there, many fellow church members did not feel that way about us. Despite our patient pastor's best efforts at explanation and peacemaking, some parishioners soon made it known that such attire was completely inappropriate at church on Sunday mornings!

In time we youth cleaned up our act a bit, the irate parishioners toned down their complaints a bit, and an uneasy compromise ensued. But we continued to feel judged for our fashion choices and hampered in our worship style. Ultimately we left that good church to seek a place where we could freely express our fashion preferences and more radical (but biblically supportable) mode of worship.

> Youth who feel judged for their personal appearance or taste in clothing will not return to the place where that judgment lingers.

We would never recommend or condone fashions that are plainly immodest or violate the consciences of those in authority over their youth. But there are plenty of morally neutral ways of dress that ought to be acceptable in a youth-friendly church environment. An atmosphere of judgment grieves the Spirit and makes religion out of real liberty in Christ. Youth who feel judged for their personal appearance or taste in clothing will not return to the place where that judgment lingers. It is therefore imperative that church leaders who want to make their church youth-friendly carefully instruct their adult members to be like the Lord, who looks at the heart, not the outward appearance (1 Sam. 16:7). Fashion styles of youth may or may not change as they mature, but adult condemnation of those styles will certainly not draw youth to Christ.

Get Lost!
I don't mean this unkindly, but your presence in the room where your kids are trying to learn to worship freely will almost always be counterproductive. That will change as they mature in the Lord. But when they are just beginning to become passionate about Jesus, your presence with them will almost certainly create an obstacle to their approach to God.

When I was a teenager, I remember how completely I wanted to shield the true aspects of myself from my father. A domineering, negative man whose primary goal in raising me was to make certain my thoughts and deeds turned out to be exactly like his, Dad was not a safe man to be around. I learned very early in life that to express my own opinions was dangerous and could easily provoke an onslaught of name-calling and vicious criticism of my youthful ideas. I vowed early in my life that I would never let Dad see the true me; sadly that vow lasted for nearly fifty years. By the Lord's grace, Dad and I reached a kind of peace before He passed away in 1997, yet my desire to hide my true self from my own father was a predictable consequence of his parenting flaws.

Perhaps your parenting flaws have been like my dad's. So perhaps for this reason — or another — your offspring find it difficult to allow their real selves to emerge in your presence. This is why parents may have to "get lost" when their kids are learning how to find their way to love, worship, and follow the Lord on their own. The Lord's goal is that the fathers' (parents') hearts be turned to their children, but that may take some time. Your children may need to form much of their spiritual identity away from your parental presence.

The same truth holds for church leaders attending youth church meetings. Youth often transfer problems they have with parents to adult leaders in their church. So, after we've mentored and placed into leadership qualified youth who are strong in Christ, the best thing we parents and church leaders can do as they meet is "get lost!"

What Do You Think?

Adults
Step one in developing a youth-led youth church is getting your church leadership on board. Do you think your church leadership is truly ready to embrace the notion that youth can minister?

If not, can you think of ways to gently nudge them in that direction?

Can you identify one or more trusted young people who could serve as a leadership core in your church's youth church?

Can you identify one or more adults to serve as behind-the-scenes overseeing coaches for the youth church?

Is it time now to take some practical steps toward the formation of a youth church in your church? If you conclude "no," the immediate action required is prayer — for God to start to give a "ministering youth" vision to those who need to receive it. If you conclude "yes," the immediate action required is still prayer. Pray for wisdom to implement successfully the vision God has imparted. What do you think would work best as a practical strategy to begin to implement a youth church in your local congregation? Gather those with hearts who share this vision and have the authority to get it done. Then start on the adventure!

Conclusion

In Isa. 43:19, the Lord says:

> "Behold, I will do something new, now
> it will spring forth; will you not be
> aware of it? I will make a roadway in
> the wilderness, rivers in the desert."

"Behold," says the Lord, to arrest our attention. By using that word He tells us: "Open your eyes, look around you, give your full concentration to what is spoken!" But why should we pay such close attention? Because He is doing something new, something unlike what has been beforehand — something unfamiliar and perhaps unrecognized at first as deriving from Him. It is in the process of emergence, of springing forth as a young plant from bare ground.

God is always doing something new. Always a fresh creative move of His Spirit is in process somewhere in the earth. He is doing His part. Our challenge is to recognize His new work, to be aware of that as-yet-indefinable, sometimes chaotically appearing new wineskin He is fashioning to contain the coming outpouring of His Spirit. "Will we not see it?" He asks. This question is His challenge to us as we consider the future of the Church.

Indeed He is making a roadway in the barren wilderness of contemporary youth culture. In the spiritual desert of the Joshua generation He is bringing forth rivers of the Water of Life. A roadway and rivers - a structure and a flow — a wineskin and new wine — these are the promises of God to those who cry to Him for a Kingdom harvest more vast than has ever been! The Joshua Generation is now being released in fervor and fearlessness to win their peers for Christ.

> He is making a roadway in the barren wilderness of contemporary youth culture. In the spiritual desert of the Joshua generation He is bringing forth rivers of the Water of Life.

As the new shape of Church emerges into the next century, will we who have been raised in the old ways be able to embrace it? We must cry to the Lord not to miss what He's doing. We must ask Him to help us to "put our spiritual glasses on," as the ECA worship team exhorts us in one of their spiritual songs. We must no longer see youth among us through the eyes of our flesh but through the eyes of His Spirit. If we can do it right, the anointing the Moses Generation enjoys from God can flow as help and blessing to our offspring so they can go in His service far beyond what we have accomplished!

To members of the Moses Generation, we exhort you: Be unceasing in prayer until your youth become zealous for Jesus. Value and nurture the God-given spiritual potential in their souls. Learn the ways of their culture so you can relevantly share Christ with them. Cultivate and praise their gifts and accomplishments. Open your own spirituality to their observation. Believe God can minister with authority through them. Trust them unless they give you cause not to. Give them space to develop their own approach to God. Invite them to participate in adult church ministries. Regard them as honorable partners with you in church life.

> We must no longer see youth among us through the eyes of our flesh but through the eyes of His Spirit.

To members of the Joshua Generation, we exhort you: Respect Christian adults; they have much to give you as mentors, much to teach you from their years in God that will help you build your ministries in the Kingdom. Adults can be your friends if you will let them. They are like normal people, just a little older! Value and honor them, and they will value and honor you. If they offer you places of ministry alongside them, say "yes!" Don't fear to ask them for what you need to start your own youth church. Share your vision with them and request their help in reaching it. Don't let your vision die as you enter increasingly into adult responsibilities. Never be ashamed of the Gospel or of proclaiming Christ in radical, bold ways. Above all, know that you are a chosen